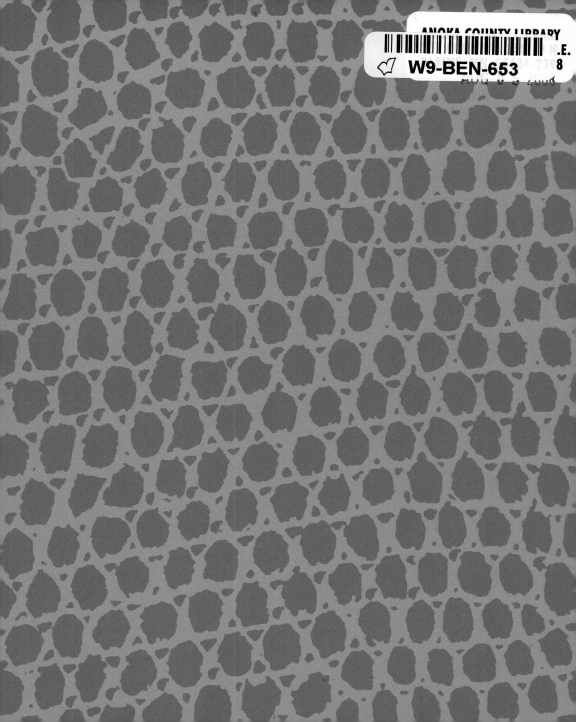

W9-BEN-653
8

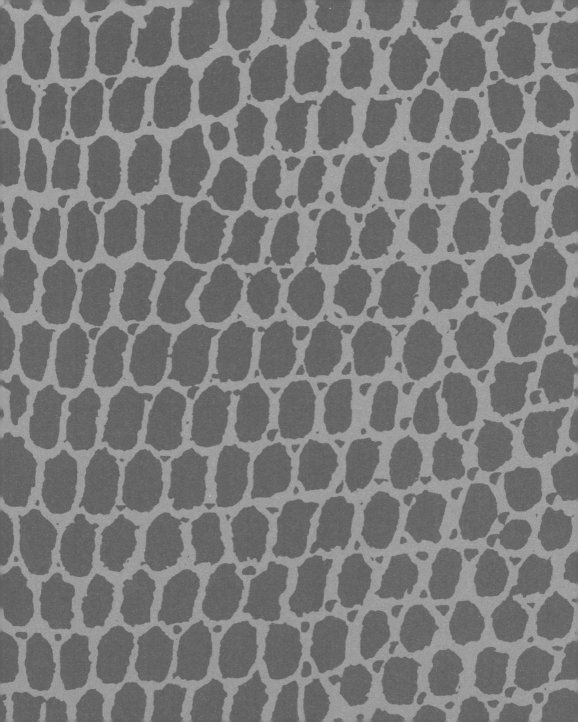

Bugs As Pets

JAY F. HEMDAL

Bugs As Pets
Project Team
Editor: Tom Mazorlig
Copy Editor: Stephanie Fornino
Indexer: Ann W. Truesdale
Interior Design: Leah Lococo Ltd. and Stephanie Krautheim
Design Layout: Stephanie Krautheim

T.F.H. Publications
President/CEO: Glen S. Axelrod
Executive Vice President: Mark E. Johnson
Publisher: Christopher T. Reggio
Production Manager: Kathy Bontz

T.F.H. Publications, Inc.
One TFH Plaza
Third and Union Avenues
Neptune City, NJ 07753

Discovery Communications, Inc. Book Development Team
Marjorie Kaplan, President, Animal Planet Media
Carol LeBlanc, Vice President, Licensing
Elizabeth Bakacs, Vice President, Creative Services
Brigid Ferraro, Director, Licensing
Peggy Ang, Vice President, Animal Planet Marketing
Caitlin Erb, Licensing Specialist

Printed and bound in China.
07 08 09 10 1 3 5 7 9 8 6 4 2

Library of Congress Cataloging-in-Publication Data
Hemdal, Jay F., 1959-
  Bugs as pets / Jay F. Hemdal.
     p. cm. – (Animal planet pet care library)
  Includes index.
  ISBN 978-0-7938-3794-6 (alk. paper)
  1. Insects as pets. I. Title.

SF459.I5H46 2008
638–dc22
                        2007035809

The Leader in Responsible Animal Care for Over 50 Years!®

www.tfh.com

CENTRAL
Garden & Pet

Table of Contents

Chapter 1

Why Keep

Bugs?

Virtually every child has at one time captured a *bug* (an insect or other terrestrial arthropod) and kept it in a jar for closer observation. While this may be educational for the child, most of these animals cannot survive for long in that sort of container. This book takes that fascination with insects to the next level, detailing how to successfully keep these animals in captivity for their entire life spans, and in some cases, even how to reproduce them and raise their offspring.

Once any initial fear of bugs by your family is overcome, the benefits of keeping these animals in captivity become clear: No other group of animals shows the diversity of living things as do insects and related arthropods. They can be kept in small spaces, do not require too much care, and are usually silent and odor-free. Bugs are perfect pets for people with limited space.

Definition of a Bug

This book covers the captive care requirements for a variety of land-dwelling invertebrates (animals without backbones). Some of these species are true insects; some are true bugs; and others are spiders, scorpions, or millipedes. The term *terrestrial arthropod* (a land-dwelling invertebrate with jointed legs) covers all of these species but is time consuming to write repeatedly. *Insect* really only includes those species of true insect, while *bug* is actually a small group of animals within the larger group of insects. However, just for the sake of variety, to change things up, throughout this book the terms *bugs*, *animals*, and *creatures* may all be used interchangeably as general terms for all terrestrial arthropods. If the term *insect* is used, it only applies to the true insects. The term *true bug* is used when discussing the insects in the family Hemiptera. The myriapods consist of the centipedes and millipedes, while the arachnids include spiders, scorpions, and associated species.

Taxonomy

Scientists have grouped all living things into categories of related organisms. This *taxonomy* tells people the relative degree to which species are related

Bugs make good pets because they are often easy to care for and take up little space. This is a baby lubber grasshopper.

Basic Classes of Terrestrial Arthropods

Class	Main Body Structure	Number of Legs	Number of Antennae	Wings Present?
Crustaceans (crabs and shrimps)	Cephalothorax and abdomen	Ten	Four	No wings
Myriapods (centipedes and millipedes)	Head and trunk (body)	Many; one or two pairs per trunk segment	Two	No wings
Arachnids (spiders, scorpions)	Cephalothorax (head) and abdomen	Eight	None	No wings
Insects (true insects)	Head, thorax, and abdomen	Six	Two	Usually has wings, but some species are wingless

to one another. Students spend entire semesters in college learning the taxonomy of insects in entomology class. The following information is a condensed version of this very complicated topic.

Every species of living creature is given a scientific name by taxonomists. While an animal may have a variety of common names (for example, lightning bug, firefly, glow bug, etc.), there is only one valid scientific name for each species (for example, *Photuris pyralis*). Most of these names are what is called a binomial—they have two parts. The first is the genus name (e.g. *Photuris*). There can be anywhere from one

to thousands of distinct species that belong to a single genus. The second is the species name (e.g. *pyralis*). In some cases where there are organisms that are more closely related than two different species, there may be a third name, the subspecies name.

Knowing basic taxonomy is helpful to the home bug keeper because it can give information about the care of animals that you have not yet kept. For example, if you know that a black widow spider (*Latrodectus mactans*) has a venomous bite, you might also want to avoid handling a red widow spider (*Latrodectus bishopi*) because they belong to the same genus and so you know that they are related. Likewise, if you already know what to feed *Eudicella smithi*, a species of flower beetle, you have a good starting point on what to try to feed *Eudicella gralli*, a different species in the same genus.

The Fascination With Insects

The sheer diversity of insects and terrestrial arthropods is the primary reason so many people find them fascinating (or in some cases,

FAMILY-FRIENDLY TIP

A Pet for All Ages

There are so many different species of insects, and their care requirements vary so much, that there is always some type that would make a suitable pet for children or adults of just about any age. Having a pet develops a sense of responsibility in the pet owner, but some pets (dogs, cats, or horses, for example) require a lot of time and effort. Younger children may find that pet bugs offer them a better way to learn to develop a lifelong appreciation for pets. Older children may be attracted to the grotesque tarantulas, scorpions, and millipedes. Adults may discover that collecting rare species of bugs is an exciting hobby.

revolting!). There are tiny insects that live in melting snow and others that live in scorching desert sands. Some insects fly, others can swim, and some can do both. Some insects are long and slender, growing to 14 inches (356 mm) in length; some beetles are huge and massive, weighing almost 1/4 pound (113 g). The only habitat that is not fully exploited by insects is the ocean's great depths.

Because of this diversity, terrestrial arthropods also vary greatly in their suitability as captive pets. Some species (for example, mayflies and some moths) do not feed at all in their adult stage. The adults live only to reproduce and then they die. Obviously, they do not make very suitable pets. Some cicadas live for 17 years as grubs, which is longer than most house pets, until you realize that they spend this time buried in the soil. Nobody enjoys a pet that they never get to see!

Which Species Is Right for You?

Studying insects in the wild or reading natural history books about them is the first step in learning about these fascinating creatures. Each person is going to find interest in different species of bugs. When it comes to bugs as pets, some people are attracted to the monstrous appearance of some species; others are more interested in beautiful colors or interesting behaviors. Obviously, by reading this book, you already have a basic interest in terrestrial arthropods.

Choosing which bug will make the best pet for you is a question you need

You can collect many bugs that make good pets, such as katydids, right in your backyard.

to answer before you get one. Keeping any animal in captivity means that you must make sure that it is healthy and housed under proper conditions. If you cannot supply an animal with its basic needs, please do not acquire it. If you tend to lose interest in new hobbies, you may find it better to keep your bugs only on a temporary basis (as explained in Chapter 2). If you want to maintain bugs for longer periods but do not want to become involved in breeding them, select a long-lived species such as a tarantula, scorpion, or giant millipede. Other people find that raising colonies of insects, such as Madagascar hissing cockroaches, gives them the most satisfaction. Read through this book very carefully; the information it contains will help you make a better decision about the type of bugs you acquire. Finally, you must never keep venomous bugs in households with children present (or perhaps even keep them at all).

Insects and the Law

There are a few instances in which a person keeping insects as pets may actually break some law or regulation without even knowing it. Ignorance of the law is no excuse, so be certain that you are aware of any laws that might affect you and your pets. There are two basic concerns: keeping live insects that are considered potential "plant pests" and those bugs that are considered endangered and thus have laws protecting them. For the most part, the only problems you may come across with endangered species are a few dishonest individuals who attempt to sell endangered butterflies (dried and mounted) to collectors.

Laws about what species of insect you can legally keep can be very complicated. In the United States, for example, it is illegal to import or own any live, exotic (from another country), true insect without a permit from the United States Department

Quick Guide to a Bug's Keeping Difficulty

Easy	Challenging	Impossible
Aquatic insects	Assassin bugs	Ants (as a colony)
Asian mantis	Bees (honeybee colony)	Butterflies (as adults)
Crickets	*Extatosoma* stick insects	Cicadas
Darkling beetles	Giant centipedes	Dragonflies (as adults)
Emperor scorpion	Grasshoppers (as a colony)	Giant rhino beetles
Giant millipedes	Land hermit crabs	Leaf insects (*Phyllium*)
House centipedes	Mexican red-leg tarantula	Lightning bugs
House spiders	Tailless whip scorpions	Mosquitoes
Madagascar hissing roach	Tropical mantids	Moths
Most temporary species	Vinegaroons	Wasps

of Agriculture Animal Plant Health Inspection Service Plant Pest Quarantine (USDA APHIS PPQ). This law helps to protect our environment from the accidental (or intentional) release of insects that could become pests in this country. In some cases, the concern is not so much with the insect itself becoming released but with the fact that the insect might have some parasite that could cause problems in our environment. At this time, the USDA does not regulate the trade in noninsect terrestrial arthropods such as tarantulas, millipedes, and scorpions.

Some states also regulate the trade in live arthropods; three that have very restrictive laws right now are Hawaii, Tennessee, and Florida. Because these laws change frequently, always check your state agricultural office or department of natural resources before bringing any exotic terrestrial arthropods into your state.

One final issue is the shipping of live terrestrial arthropods: Even if there are no laws regulating the movement of a particular arthropod between two locations, you must ensure that the carrier (postal service, airfreight company, etc.) is aware that the shipment contains live animals and that the shipment meets all of its requirements in terms of how it is packaged, how long the shipment time will be, etc.

How Best to Determine Local Insect Laws?

Due to the many layers of wildlife laws (local, state, national, and international), it can be very difficult to figure out which laws apply to you and your pets. The Internet is probably not the best source for this information—the laws frequently change, and some people on the Internet post information without checking it well. One possible resource is your local zoo, aquarium, or insectarium. These organizations always follow local laws, and they can usually give you an updated list of regulations that apply in your region. Remember, these laws were made to keep you and the environment safe from insects that might escape and cause environmental damage.

Acquiring Insects

Acquiring high-quality terrestrial arthropods is the most important step in maintaining their continued good health. Because little is known about diseases of arthropods, and because the environment in which an animal has been housed has such a strong bearing on its health, you must start with the best-quality animals that you can. There are a few different ways one can acquire pet bugs. Obviously, catching your own is one possibility, but purchasing them from a dealer is the usual way to acquire the more exotic species. Some insect aficionados actually set up trades with other people, which helps to reduce the cost of the transaction. Always be certain that you acquire your animals through legal and ethical means.

Be sure to follow the law when collecting bugs; some species are protected, including several butterflies.

Thoughts on Handling

One of the enjoyable things about having a pet is interacting with it—for example, playing catch with a dog or giving catnip to a cat. Some pet bugs, such as tarantulas, butterflies, and assassin bugs, are strictly "hands off." Other bugs, such as giant millipedes, can easily be handled with proper care. Always know how your pets will react to handling; grasshoppers will often try to jump away, while some mantises may pinch your finger. While bugs cannot learn to do tricks or anything like that, some do become used to handling, allowing you to hold them and observe them more closely. Some people in Japan keep giant beetles as pets and buy their animals fancy metal body ornaments and even tiny collars and leashes!

Purchasing animals through a pet dealer is one of the best ways to get a good variety as well as appropriate care information. Some dealers do not regularly stock bugs, but most can order them for you. Pet stores are also good sources for supplies and live foods, such as crickets. In some cases, you may be able to raise bugs and sell some of your excess back to local pet stores.

Collecting bugs around your own home is certainly the most cost effective means to acquire them. However, keep in mind that because the animals will be familiar to you, they may lack some of the allure of exotic species. The following are some methods that can be employed to capture live bugs.

By Hand

Certainly requiring the least investment in terms of equipment, some bugs can be captured by hand. The three drawbacks are that many insects are simply too quick, some species react to hand capture with defensive methods such as stinging, and finally—even if done carefully—hand capture may injure more delicate

It is very easy to injure small bugs, so be careful when you collect them.

bugs. Do some research ahead of time to determine what species in your area should not be captured by hand. Hand capture is definitely the most selective technique; you sight the animal you want and then simply pick it up.

By Net

A variety of nets can be used to collect live bugs, usually with little damage. The typical butterfly net is made of very lightweight material and is used to capture flying insects while "on the wing." Dip nets have heavy frames and sturdy netting and are used to capture aquatic insects. Sweep nets are larger nets made of cloth and are used, as their name implies, to sweep vegetation to capture insects. One of the least selective capture techniques, sweep nets can be used to capture smaller insects to serve as food for animals in your main collection.

Very similar to a net, a beating tray is a large piece of cloth held out between two sticks. The tray is held open underneath some promising vegetation, and as the plant is shaken, insects may fall out and into the tray. This works well in capturing stick insects and other species that typically do not fly.

By Trap

Pitfalls are buckets with smooth sides buried into the soil up to their tops. As insects scurry along (especially at night), they tend to fall into the trap. Because some species can crawl right back out, you may need to check the trap frequently. In some cases, a ring of smooth, slippery packing tape attached around the inside of the trap near the top will keep bugs from crawling back out too easily. Using different types of bait may attract more insects to the pitfall but also may attract unwanted scavengers, such as mice. Light traps work well at night, taking advantage of the attraction many insects have to a light source. Simply rig a white light behind a stretched white cloth such as a bedsheet, and net insects off the material as they are attracted to the light behind it.

Preserved Insect Collections

While some people are interested in keeping living bugs as pets, there are actually many more people whose hobby is building collections of dried and pinned insects. Some species of

13

Some Protected Species

- American burying beetle
- birdwing butterflies
- *Brachypelma* tarantulas
- cape stag beetle
- Corsican swallowtail butterfly
- emperor scorpion
- *Homerus* swallowtail butterflies
- Karner blue butterfly
- Luzon peacock swallowtail
- *Partula* land snails
- *Zayante* band-winged grasshoppers

Some bugs, such as lady-bugs, are difficult to keep alive in captivity. Observe them for a day or two and then let them go.

bugs are virtually impossible to keep alive in captivity for any amount of time because their life cycle is too complicated or their diet is too difficult to supply. These same animals can more easily be kept as permanent displays as nonliving examples. In fact, professional entomologists rely almost entirely on collections of dried bugs to produce their collections of different species. These preserved animals, properly mounted, look just as realistic as the living organism. The only difference is that one cannot learn anything about the life cycle or habits of a dead, preserved bug. Still, there may come a time when one of your pets dies, and rather than just disposing of it, you may decide to mount it for future observation and study.

There are two basic methods used to create preserved insects for a study collection: dried and mounted on a pin, or for soft-bodied animals, preserved in a solution of 70 percent ethyl alcohol. The basic supplies needed for an insect collection include the following:

- forceps and teasing needles
- insect pins of various diameters
- magnifying glass or loupe
- paper labels and a fine pen (to record specimen data)
- pinning block (to achieve the proper height of the insects on the pins)
- riker boxes (glass fronted, to display the insect collection, with foam bottom)
- relaxing jar (moist sand covered by a piece of cardboard in a jar)
- spreading board (needed to effectively mount butterflies and moths)

To begin, an appropriate-sized insect pin is passed through the dead insect's body (usually through the thorax, and typically just to the right of the centerline). Small insects may be first lightly glued to a triangle of paper, which in turn is mounted on the insect pin. All good insect collections must be labeled. Essential information for the labels includes the following:

- date
- country of origin
- state or territory
- locality data (nearest major landmark)
- collector's name
- habitat information
- common name
- scientific name (if known)
- family

Making a *Pooter*—A Bug Collector With a Funny Name

One method to collect small bugs is by using an aspirator. Entomologists sometimes call this device a *pooter*. These gentle suction devices consist of a clear vial with a two-hole rubber stopper in it. To each of these holes you attach a short piece of rigid tubing, to which is attached a longer piece of rubber tubing. The rigid tubing must extend through the stopper into the vial. Cover the end of one of these tubes with a piece of screen or cheesecloth. (This prevents you from sucking bugs or dirt into your mouth when you use the device.) When a bug is located, simply extend one of the tubes near it, and gently suck in on the other one (with the screen on it!). With practice, you will find it easy to capture insects. Obviously, this only works as a method to collect very small species—and some hobbyists find that pooters are really most useful for collecting live insect food to feed their main pets.

Photography is another way to "preserve" your insect collection. Due to the small size of most insects, a camera with a macro lens is required. Many people now choose digital cameras over film, although some purists and professionals still rely on the latter. For a good digital camera to use in photographing insects, look for the macro ability and a resolution of five or more megapixels. Camera shake can really blur photos taken in macro mode, so a sturdy tripod is important. In some cases, the built-in flash of the camera leaves a shadow on the image when used in close macro mode. To get around this, use supplemental light sources and bypass the camera flash, or buy an add-on flash that sits up higher on the camera.

A Record of Your Pets

Keeping a written record (called a logbook) about the pet insects you have kept will help you learn what methods worked well for what species and what things did not work well. Think of a logbook as a diary for your pets. You should write down the date you acquired the animal, what it likes to eat, any interesting habits it has, etc. Another important thing to keep track of is how the animal looks. You can do this by taking pictures of it, but you may find that drawing your pet's portrait is a better method. By drawing a picture of an insect, you will need to take a lot of time to study it carefully, and you will therefore learn a lot more about the animal. Besides, it is always more fun to have a picture that you made yourself!

15

Why Keep Bugs?

Chapter 2

A Bug's Life

What are the basic things that make people happy?
A good place to live, enough food to eat, and
freedom from disease are at the top of most
people's lists. It turns out that these are exactly
the same things your pets require from you! This
chapter describes the basic needs that your pet
bugs have. Caring for an animal in captivity is
called *animal husbandry*. This chapter outlines the
basic husbandry requirements for your pet bugs.

Suitable Housing

The first step in keeping bugs as pets is to provide suitable housing for the species you intend to keep. Too often, people approach this issue backward, buying or catching an animal and then hunting around for suitable housing for it. The problem is that without careful planning, the spur-of-the-moment housing that you locate may not be what is best for the animal. Always set up the proper housing for an animal *before* you bring it home.

For terrestrial arthropods, there are some basic housing requirements that must be met, and these may vary among species. Obviously, cage size is an important factor. Too large of a cage and the animal will be difficult to see, while too small of a cage is unfair to the animal and may cause health problems. In addition to size, the actual dimension of the cage is important. A ground-dwelling species will prefer a low, flat cage, while an arboreal (tree- or plant-dwelling species) will prefer a taller cage. Substrate (bottom cover) is important for some species and can range from dry sand to moist soil. Finally, all bugs have specific temperature and humidity (water vapor content) needs for the air that surrounds them.

Location

You need to determine the best location for your pet bug's enclosure well in advance of actually setting it up. Criteria to consider regarding cage placement include room temperature (will it allow the cage to remain within the proper range?) and light levels. Some bugs are nocturnal, and if kept in a container in a brightly lit room, may not be visible during the daytime. In addition, direct sunlight streaming in through a room's window may cause dramatic heat buildup inside of a small cage, possibly killing the inhabitants. Some insect cages rely on electrical

Different bugs need different types of enclosures. This stick insect from Texas needs a large, tall cage with branches for climbing.

power for heaters, humidifiers, or lights. Their location is therefore dependant on easy access to a suitable power source (preferably Ground Fault Circuit Interrupter (GFCI) protected).

Cage Types

Many types of containers can be used to house bugs. Most of these cages, like fish tanks, terrariums, jars, and glass exhibit cases, are adapted from other uses. The most obvious requirement is that the enclosure in question be able to house the bugs safely, without a chance of their escape. Secondary to that is their ability to allow you to clearly view the animals inside. Materials used in cage construction range from glass to plastic to screening and may include a combination of materials in a single container. While cages need to be able to safely and securely house your pets, they must also be able to give you easy access for cleaning and feeding them.

Pet stores or entomological supply companies generally offer the best-quality housing for your pet bugs. Toy stores may sell insect cages, but some of these products are better suited for temporary housing rather than long-

The Expert Knows

Environmental Control for Multiple Cages

Avid bug keepers may reach a point where it becomes difficult to maintain proper environmental levels in each individual cage they have. Assuming that the animals being kept all have the same general requirements, it is usually much easier to place a number of cages inside one larger container (or even a small room) and then control the humidity, ventilation, lighting, and temperature of that one area. In addition, the larger container can serve as secondary containment. Should any creature escape its primary enclosure, it would remain inside the larger container. Remember that although it is a great time and labor saver to have a number of insect cages being controlled from one point, if there is an equipment malfunction of some sort (a sticking thermostat, burned-out heater, etc.) all of the animals will be affected. Still, most zoos and insectariums maintain their arthropod collections in this manner.

term habitats. Using a little ingenuity, you may find that there are many other containers that can house your pets, including a wide variety of household jars and sturdy boxes.

Small fish tanks work well for housing many types of terrestrial arthropods, but take care in selecting a screen top for the tank because some of the ones on the market are not really designed to keep small insects in their place. Making your own aquarium lid is often the best solution. The simplest method is to build a wooden frame slightly larger than the rim of the tank and attach a panel of aluminum window screening to it. Then, the weight of the wood frame will hold the screen tightly against the top edge of the tank. Be aware that some bugs are capable of biting through plastic window screen, so metal screen is best.

One problem with full screen tops is that they do not hold in the humidity that some animals require. For those creatures, cutting a piece of plastic sheet to fit the inside trim of the aquarium will work. Holes can then be drilled in the top and covered with screen to allow some ventilation. Plexiglas tends to deform and gap over time, so it does not always make a secure tank lid for insects. A better material to use is something called polycarbonate structured sheet or "double wall hollow channel sheet," available online or locally from specialty plastics distributors. This lightweight clear material does not bow or bend over time. It can be cut

to fit easily, and screened vents can be added as needed.

In some cases, even a tight-fitting lid is not enough to keep the bugs inside their cage. Very small species such as ants and some cockroaches can crawl under almost any type of cage lid and then escape. In these special cases, you may need to place a layer of vegetable oil, petroleum jelly, or liquid Teflon in a ring around the top of the cage. When the small insects reach this ring, they cannot cross it and so remain inside the cage where they belong. In the case of some insects such as crickets, even a ring of clear packing tape (that is too smooth for them to climb on) is enough to keep them in their cage. Remember, though, that these methods are temporary, and you will need to clean or replace the barriers occasionally to keep your pets secure in their cage.

Sometimes, mostly at insectariums, the problem is not so much the bugs escaping their cage but other insects

Grasshoppers and other gnawing bugs may be able to bite through mesh cage tops; use metal screening for these species.

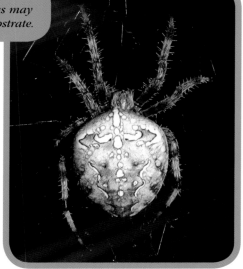

such as tiny ants getting into the cage and causing problems. One way to control this problem is to set the cage (or its supports) in a container of water. Few insects can cross the surface of open water in a container, and this keeps pest insects out of the cage while also keeping your pets securely caged. Of course, this water trick does not work for species that can swim or fly.

Substrates

The floor of most bug cages is covered with some material or another, termed the substrate. This material serves two purposes: It enhances the naturalistic appearance of the enclosure and may provide the animal being housed some specific husbandry need, such as sand to burrow in, soil to lay eggs in, etc. At the same time, substrates often increase the effort needed to properly clean the cage, and an improper substrate choice can actually harm some animals.

Throughout the species care accounts in this book, if there are specific requirements for an animal's substrate, it will be mentioned there. Otherwise, just keep in mind that a good substrate must be inexpensive, easily cleaned, and perhaps decorative. Many birds and reptiles are kept on just a layer of newspaper, which meets all the requirements except that it is not very decorative. Plain brown Kraft paper serves the same purpose but is

a bit more pleasing to the eye. Some insects (such as cockroaches and beetle larvae) are positively thigmotaxic with regard to their substrate. This means that they feel most comfortable when completely enclosed and touching the substrate, such as a cockroach that prefers to live between sheets of newspaper. A few bugs, like butterflies, leaf insects, and praying mantises, are negatively thigmotaxic, meaning they prefer to stay away from the substrate. For these bugs, a bare cage floor may work best and will certainly make cleaning easier.

Temperature and Humidity

All bugs have specific needs in terms of air temperature and humidity. A few species even have different needs at various points of their life

Insect Cage Cover Types

Here is a summary of the pros and cons of various cage covers.

Type	Pros	Cons
Cloth	Retains very small creatures	Does not hold humidity, opaque, can be chewed on
Fiberglass screen	Inexpensive, widely available	Does not hold humidity, some larger animals will chew on it
Flexible plastic sheet	Inexpensive, holds humidity well	Not durable
Glass	Clear, holds humidity well	Fragile, minimal air flow
Hybrid (e.g., plastic with screen opening)	Combines the best features of other types	Usually needs to be constructed by the pet owners
Plastic egg crate	Easily cut to fit, sturdy	Can only be used for larger animals
Plastic molded lids with screening	Inexpensive, widely available	May not fit tightly enough to hold small insects
Solid plastic sheet	Clear, holds humidity very well	May warp over time
Stainless steel screen	Very durable, available in many mesh sizes	Expensive

cycles. The species accounts in the following chapters give specific recommendations for the humidity and temperature requirements of the bugs under discussion. It is always best to devise a way to control these two parameters when keeping bugs. That way, levels can be adjusted to fit the changing needs of the animals, or they can be changed if you choose to house a different species in the cage.

Air takes up heat rapidly and loses heat just as quickly. Water, on the other hand, tends to change temperature

more slowly. Most bugs are kept in air-filled cages, where cage temperatures can change rapidly, possibly to the point of harming them. For example, an insect cage sitting on a windowsill in a home might be at 65°F (18.3°C) in the morning, but when direct sunlight hits the cage in the afternoon, the temperature could quickly rise to over 100°F (37.8°C).

The standard means to heat insect cages is by using an incandescent or infrared lamp (a bulb that produces heat with a red or blue light). Most people adjust the distance of the lamp from the cage to control the temperature inside the cage. Care must be taken not to overheat the animals by placing the heat source too close to them. Advanced insect hobbyists use a thermostatic controller that turns the heat lamp on and off as needed to maintain the proper temperature inside the cage. Thermostats suitable for this purpose are sometimes sold in pet store reptile departments.

Water can be introduced into the air of a cage to boost humidity, while air conditioning or dehumidification may be required to reduce the humidity of the air for certain desert species. In many cases, spraying a mist of water into a cage will temporarily raise the humidity of the air space in the enclosure. Covering the same cage with an impermeable material (but still allowing some fresh air in) will help to retain that moisture.

One problem is that there are some tropical insects that require high humidity but do not do well in the stagnant environment of a cage that is closed off to artificially boost the humidity. Mold may grow on the animals or their eggs, the food left out for them may spoil too fast, or they may even develop bacterial or parasitic infections. In such cases, it may be necessary to raise the humidity of an entire room and then place open screen cages inside that room, which will allow the airflow that some insects need. Live plants might help to maintain humidity, but they are difficult to care for in a terrarium if they don't receive enough light. In humid terrariums, bacteria may grow that could cause human health problems if ingested—so always wash your hands after handling your animals or cleaning their cages.

Fans are also useful for moving air around in cages and for removing excess moisture from cages. Remember, however, that evaporation is a cooling process, and fans may lower the air temperature of the cages too far.

Suitable Cage Decorations for Terrestrial Arthropods

Here is a summary of the different cage decorations and their properties:

Cage Decorations	Pros	Cons
Branches	Easily acquired, can be trimmed to fit, easy to replace	Difficult to clean, may rot if kept wet
Ceramic structures (e.g., clay flowerpots)	Long lasting, easily cleaned	Unnatural appearance
Cholla cactus skeleton	Provides good hiding places; looks natural in desert terrariums	Expensive, may rot if kept wet
Cork bark	Rot resistant, available in flat sheets, tubes, and other shapes	Expensive
Driftwood	Readily available at pet stores	May absorb water
Flat rocks	Can be used to make caves	May injure or kill animals if the rocks shift or fall
Live plants	Very naturalistic, may help to maintain humidity level	Require light and regular watering to stay alive, difficult to clean
Manzanita branches	Attractive, rot resistant	Expensive
Plastic artificial rocks	Long lasting, lightweight	Expensive, may not look natural
Plastic plants	Very durable, easily cleaned	Not always natural looking
Silk plants	Very natural looking	Expensive, difficult to clean

Cage Decorations

Cage decorations or furniture is not only used to make the cage look more natural for humans—they also benefit the animals themselves. Insects kept in a bare cage may suffer from stress if their normal habit is to hide under something or to climb on a branch. Web-building spiders will suffer if they do not have suitable upright branches to use as attachment points for their webs. Certain species need to burrow in some substrate, so this substance may be considered cage furniture for them. Material for use inside an insect cage must be nontoxic, waterproof, and easily cleaned (or replaced as needed).

In a Pickle Jar: Native Insects

So many youngsters have kept bugs in jars that they have become almost an accepted cage type. However, the basic pickle jar has some drawbacks. Using a nail to poke holes in the lid often leaves jagged edges, the glass jar is not optically perfect (it distorts the view of the animal inside), and the pickle smell (or the smell of whatever the jar originally contained) is difficult to wash out. Still, "in a pickle jar" is meant to describe keeping a terrestrial arthropod in a small, inexpensive container for a short time.

Some species of bug are simply not suited for long-term captivity. Even those, however, can be kept for a day to a week in a small container for observation. At the end of that time, the animal should be released where it was found. The key to keeping the bug in a jar is to follow some simple rules.

FAMILY-FRIENDLY TIP

Your Pet's Safety

Keep in mind that just as you are interested in pet bugs, small children may be as well. You need to keep your pet bugs in a safe place, where little kids will not accidentally harm them. Children are naturally curious, and unlike heavy fish aquariums, insect cages often can easily be lifted up and moved around by even small children.

In some cases, just making sure that the cages are kept out of reach of children or pets is enough of a precaution. Remember, though, that some kids simply take it as a personal challenge when something is moved beyond their reach. One way to deal with inquisitive kids is to let them become familiar with the animals. If they have good supervised access to the bugs, they are less likely to get into mischief with them when you are not around. In some instances, the best solution may be to anchor the cage to a shelf or table using brackets. Obviously, any cage housing a bug that is capable of biting or causing harm to humans must have a locking lid if kept in a home with children present.

25

A Bug's Life

These rules include keeping the jar out of direct sunlight, only adding one animal per jar (unless you are certain that they will peacefully coexist), and adding just enough moisture that the animal does not dehydrate but not so much that mold forms. A small bit of sponge or wadded-up paper towel soaked in tap water serves as a sufficient water source in most cases. Remember that some insects do not recognize water in a dish; they need to have a fine mist of water sprayed into the cage for them to drink, as they would drink dew out in the wild.

Mixed-Species Terrariums

In some instances, people may wish to create a "mini environment" for their pets, a mixed-species terrarium containing a variety of plants, bugs, and perhaps other animals. The obvious problem facing people in this task is

Insects Best Suited for Short-Term Captivity

- Ants (unless a colony can be started with a queen)
- Backswimmers (in a jar with water, of course)
- Caterpillars
- Cicadas
- Flies (except easily cultured species such as fruit flies)
- Fungus beetles
- Lady beetles (difficult to feed adults)
- Stag beetles (adults feed on plant sap)
- Tiger beetles
- Velvet ants
- Wasps

that many animals are predators of one another and simply cannot be successfully housed together in a small container. Mixed-species environments are always more difficult to maintain than ones housing individual animals or even single species. For example, a particular bug may have different temperature or humidity requirements than do the live plants chosen to outfit its terrarium. Some insects such as stick insects and grasshoppers may feed

Many bugs, such as mantises, eat other bugs, so mixing species is not recommended.

on plants used to decorate their enclosures. Finally, mixed-species exhibits with natural soil substrate are difficult to clean, and waste products from the animals may build up in the soil.

Animal Escapes

While generally not life threatening, many people have severe phobias (irrational fears) about many species of insects and spiders. Unless you suffer from a phobia yourself, it is unlikely that you can imagine the terror these people face when confronted with one of the animals that they fear. For this reason (among others, of course), it is vitally important that all of the cages that you use to house your pet bugs are completely escape proof. Insects loose in a house will surely cause problems, especially for those who are frightened of them.

Some keepers like to play practical jokes on others with their bug pets by chasing after people with them or leaving them to run loose in a room. This is not "just good fun"—it can truly scare people, and the extra handling of the bug can cause it health problems. (Tarantulas are known to die from rupturing their abdomens if dropped even a few feet [less than a meter] from a person's hand onto a hard surface.)

Health Issues

Your local veterinarian is not likely to be skilled in identifying and treating

Commensalism

Commensal organisms are those that live on another species but do not cause harm to that other species, as a parasite would. One commonly seen commensal organism is a tiny mite that is often found on giant African millipedes. These can simply be wiped off the body with a cloth if they become too numerous. No chemical control is possible because any compound that is capable of killing the mites will also harm the distantly related millipedes.

diseases of pet bugs. You will therefore need to teach yourself how to identify and treat any common diseases your animals may develop. Luckily, bugs are very resilient animals that rarely develop disease problems if kept in proper conditions.

Diseases

Very little is known about infectious diseases of terrestrial arthropods kept as pets. The best most people can expect to do is maintain the animal in the best environment possible in the hopes that the creature's own immune system can fend off any bacterial or protozoal diseases. Certainly, newly collected animals that may be harboring diseases should not be mixed with your existing collection

African giant millipedes often have a number of mites living on them; these mites are completely harmless.

in those creatures as well as the intended outdoor pests.

Metazoan Parasites

Metazoan parasites are multi-cellular organisms that attack other multi-cellular creatures. Common examples include tapeworms in dogs or mosquitoes on humans. Only a few metazoan parasites of insects are known to be an issue, and these are parasitic mites that can decimate honeybee hives. The difficulty in treating this sort of disease is that because both the host animal and the parasite are metazoans, any

unless they have been quarantined for some time. The difficulty, of course, is knowing how long to quarantine a new animal. Many aquarists use a quarantine period of four to six weeks for new fish, and it is probable that terrestrial arthropods may require slightly less time than that.

Bacillus thuringiensis

Bacillus thuringiensis (also known as Bt) is a gram positive soil-dwelling bacterium that can infect insects. In fact, it has been made available as a pest control product because the endotoxins the bacteria produce are not toxic to other organisms—just insects (primarily moths and beetles). Different varieties of Bt have been developed, including one type that is effective against mosquito larvae. It is possible that application of Bt near an insect collection could cause death

Household Materials That May Poison Pet Bugs

- Air fresheners
- Ammonia
- Flea bombs and treatments
- Household insecticides
- Mothballs
- Overheated Teflon pans
- Residual soaps
- Solvents (mineral spirits, Xylene, etc.)
- Tobacco smoke (in heavy amounts)

treatment that is likely to eradicate the parasite will also harm the host.

Molds

Molds are plant-like nonphotosynthetic organisms that feed on dead or decaying matter. These filamentous funguses are saprophytes—they gain their nutrition by decomposing nonliving organic material. If the insect cage is kept clean and as dry as the insects can tolerate, mold is rarely a problem for your bugs. Mold can be an issue for developing eggs, though, especially those deposited in soil. Stick insects eggs kept too moist may develop mold infections that may reduce the hatching rate. Minor mold infections can be controlled by reducing the humidity of the container. In the event of a major outbreak, the whole container may need to be disinfected with a solution of 10 percent household bleach in water (after all the animals have been removed, of course).

Poisons

Accidental poisoning can cause problems with pet terrestrial arthropods. People use a variety of chemicals in and around their homes. These cause no problem for the home's primary inhabitants (people and larger pets) but might wreak havoc with a live insect collection.

Common sense would tell a person not to use an aerosol insect killing spray anywhere near a live insect collection, but poisoning can occur through less obvious routes. For example, garden plants may be treated with a systemic insecticide that lingers in the plant tissue. If this plant material is then fed to pet insects even weeks later, it may cause their death.

Injuries

From time to time, pet arthropods may experience injuries. Most of these occur during improper handling, but injuries also can be caused by attacks from tankmates or tank decorations that have collapsed on an animal. The most common injury is when a person decides (unwisely) that they want to handle their pet, and a leg of the creature is torn off or broken while trying to extract the animal

Rose-haired and other tarantulas can be easily injured or killed in a fall, so handle them carefully or not at all.

First Aid

It is important for everyone (including kids) to know how to perform first aid. While people's reactions to insect bites and stings vary, the following first-aid process will work in most cases. Remember, when in doubt about the seriousness of the bite, call 911 or your local emergency service immediately.

- Move the person away from the animal causing the problem (without being harmed yourself!). If you are alone, let someone else know what has happened.

- If a stinger is present in the person's skin, try to scrape it out with a credit card or the back of a table knife.

- Clean the wound with hydrogen peroxide and apply an antiseptic.

- Apply a cold compress to reduce pain and swelling.

- For itching and local skin reactions, apply cream containing hydrocortisone. Some people find that oral antihistamines will help to limit minor allergic reactions.

- Immediately contact emergency personnel if any serious allergic reactions develop.

from its cage. Another common injury is damage from a fall, often when a person is holding an arthropod and accidentally drops it (often seen with tarantulas).

Many arthropods are able to constrict their lymphatic vessels (like our arteries) at the site of an injury, keeping them from bleeding to death. During subsequent molts, it is even possible for the missing appendage to at least partially grow back. However, if the damage is to the animal's abdomen, it is often fatal. Some people have reported attempts to seal off the injured exoskeleton of injured arthropods with cyanoacrylate glue (such as a fast-bonding glue or a medical glue). While often not

successful, it is worth a try because the only other option is to either euthanize the animal or simply wait to see if it can survive the injury on its own.

Longevity

The potential longevity of terrestrial arthropods varies from days (in the case of insects that do not feed in the adult stage) to more than 25 years for females of some species of tarantula. Some insects seem "hardwired" to live a predetermined length of time. For example, temperate insects that normally die during the season's first heavy frost (such as praying mantises) will usually not survive much longer than that in captivity, even when they are not exposed to cold temperatures.

If you find that certain arthropods are consistently not living as long as they would in the wild, consider modifying the care you provide, or perhaps refrain from keeping that species at all.

Safety When Handling Pet Bugs

It is doubtful that anyone begins a new hobby with the expectation of being injured while participating in it. Certainly, there are risky activities such as motorcycle racing and mountain climbing, but even participants in those sports work hard to ensure their personal safety. Keeping insects as pets as outlined in this book is about as risk-free as any activity that involves live animals. Still, because there are a few instances where uninformed hobbyists could be injured by their pet bugs, this section outlines those rare problems and offers advice as to how to avoid them.

A few terrestrial arthropods can seriously harm or even kill a human. Hobbyists should not attempt to keep these species—there are always more interesting harmless species to be had. So what is the most dangerous "bug?" Is it a black widow, the brown recluse spider, a tarantula? Nope. Worldwide, approximately 2 million people die each year from malaria, a disease transmitted by mosquitoes. On average, only four deaths per year are attributed to spider bites in the United States. Remember, if you are ever unsure about your safety when handling any animal, simply do not pick it up or allow it to leave its cage. Isolation from humans will eliminate all chance that a bug can harm you.

Allergic Reactions

Reactions to insect stings and bites can cause different reactions in different people or in the same person at different times. In a normal reaction, the person feels some pain and swelling at the site of the sting that generally lasts a few hours. In a toxic reaction (often resulting from multiple stings), the symptoms are more serious and may include headaches, intense pain, and skin changes at the site of the sting. These reactions can last for several days and should be examined by a physician. Sometimes, an allergic reaction occurs with symptoms like hives, swelling of the tongue, difficulty breathing, and dizziness. Emergency medical services need to be summoned immediately if you suspect an allergic reaction to an insect bite or sting.

Chapter 3

Feed the

Bugs

Captive bugs all require appropriate foods fed in proper quantities for their long-term health. After the environment in which the animal is kept, diet is the next most important thing. Some insects have very strict dietary requirements, while others will accept a wider variety of foods.

Some species of bugs have such stringent diets that their needs cannot be met easily. Other animals, such as the Madagascar pill millipede, have diets that are not yet known. Some insects, such as mayflies, do not even feed once they reach their adult form. This section outlines the basic dietary requirements of terrestrial arthropods; more specific dietary information will be found in later sections that provide detailed care of each species.

With most higher animals (mammals and other vertebrates), the proper amount to feed an individual can be gauged by their appearance. Overfed vertebrates become fat, while underfed animals appear thin. It is not as easy to tell if an invertebrate is receiving an appropriate amount of food. Some arthropods will show expanded body segments if they are overfed. A fat

FAMILY–FRIENDLY TIP

Feeding the Bugs

Even young children can help with the care of insect pets, and feeding them is one activity that they really enjoy. Think about it—would you rather clean up the yard after a dog or feed it treats as it does tricks? Of course, adult supervision is always important to avoid over- or underfeeding the animals. Once an adult has established a feeding routine and provided the child with simple instructions, it is easy to allow her to help.

Although they are sometimes kept as pets, crickets are the most common food item for carnivorous bugs.

Herbivorous Diets for Bugs

Common Leaf Diets	Fruits and Vegetables	Liquid Foods
Lettuce (low food value) Oak leaves (for native stick insects) Bramble (for tropical stick insects) Endive Bok-choy Spinach	Banana (a staple for many species) Apple (easy to come by) Potato (lasts for a long time) Yam and carrot Mango and papaya	Sugar water (with vitamins) Fruit juice (use 100% pure) Maple syrup (with water added)

scorpion or centipede can be identified by its swollen body, will which feature "stretch marks" between the body plates. This may cause health issues later if the food amount offered to the animal is not reduced. Most true insects will only eat enough food to maintain proper growth and will not overeat.

Food must be presented in an appropriate manner. Some predators will refuse anything but live, moving prey items. Many herbivores will not feed on plant material unless it is upright and positioned as how living plants normally grow. In all cases, uneaten food must be promptly removed to prevent spoilage that can foster the growth of mold, fungus, and bacteria, which may in turn infect the bugs. Many bugs gain most, if not all, of the moisture they need from the food they eat, and so if not fed regularly, may dehydrate and die.

Carnivorous Bugs

Carnivorous bugs eat other animals, usually other terrestrial arthropods.

Some large spiders have been reported to feed on vertebrate animals (like lizards, frogs, small mammals, and birds), but this is the exception, not the rule. Most carnivorous arthropods are predators—that is, they seek living prey. Some, such as fly larvae, feed on dead animal matter and can be considered scavengers.

By far, the most commonly used live food for pet bugs is the common house cricket, *Acheta domesticus*. These are available in many pet stores, can be ordered online, or can even be raised yourself. Usually fed alive, crickets are also available freeze dried for those animals that will accept nonliving food. Crickets are available at different ages (and thus different sizes) to serve as food for large or small animals. Another commonly used food source are the larvae of the mealworm beetle. These may not be accepted by all predatory bugs because their movement (crawling along the ground) may not set up the appropriate signal to the predator that it is a suitable food source. For very small bugs, live fruit flies can be cultured and used as food. Pet stores and Internet pet suppliers sometimes have other suitable food species available, such as springtails or silkworm larvae.

Herbivorous Insects

Some terrestrial arthropods feed on plant material and vegetables; fruits and other plants serve as food for them. There are three basic categories of herbivorous bugs: those that feed primarily on leaves, those that feed on plant sap, and those that feed on fruits, roots, or other solid plant material. Many herbivorous insects are specialized in the type of plant material they will accept as food. Some stick insects (often just called "sticks"), for example, will only feed on the leaves of certain tropical plants belonging to the rose family.

Although any plant material that is safe for human consumption *should* be safe to feed to your pet insects, some people worry that residual systemic insecticides or growth-inhibiting hormones used in these foods may adversely affect their pet bugs. To be certain that this will not be a problem, you can raise your own plants, buy certified organic vegetables, or collect your own plants from the wild (in areas free of pesticides, of course).

Live Foods

Crickets

House crickets are sold by the dozen in many pet stores for use as food for reptiles and amphibians. Most carnivorous terrestrial arthropods relish them as well. Many people buy just enough to feed immediately to their pet bugs. To store crickets for a few weeks, keep them in a secure cage with crumpled up newspaper to hide in. Offer them a bit of moistened cotton to drink from and some small bits of vegetables to eat. The cricket's constant chirping can be annoying to some people, and escaped crickets can really get around inside a person's house. Insect hobbyists sometime remove the large spiny rear legs of the crickets so that their pet bugs can more easily capture and eat the crickets. Raising

Banana is accepted by many herbivorous bugs, including this giant stag beetle.

crickets in the home can be a bit complicated, so check the Internet for different methods before choosing one to try for yourself.

Mealworms

Commonly fed to pet reptiles, mealworms are sometimes fed to predatory insects, in either their larva or adult beetle stage. They are easily reared in a covered plastic shoebox partially filled with a mixture of oatmeal and chicken laying crumbles (from a feed store) with a small amount of brewer's yeast added. If chicken laying crumbles are not available, use a mixture of whole oatmeal and cornmeal. A damp sponge or a bit of potato serves as a moisture source; this needs to be replaced whenever it starts to dry out. The life cycle from egg to adult takes three to four months. For long-term cultures, a large mesh screen can be used to separate the larvae and beetles from the old oatmeal, which is then replaced.

"Super" mealworms are the larvae of a different beetle that lives in rotting wood. These must be purchased as needed, as they are difficult to breed.

Fruit Flies

The wingless variety of fruit fly (*Drosophila*) is often cultured as a laboratory animal, but they are easy to raise in the home as well. Starter cultures and supplies are available from various biological supply houses—look for the term *apterous* (wingless) when selecting a type to buy. Be aware that winged flies sometimes come out of

Flightless fruit flies are easy to culture and are an excellent food for many small bugs.

these cultures and can become a bit of a pest if they get loose in your home.

To begin an active culture of fruit flies, you will need a dozen small containers with fine mesh lids, a starter culture of the flies themselves, and some prepared growing media. The media is prepared and added to the bottom of some of the containers. A bit of large mesh plastic screen propped up inside the container provides a spot for the adult flies to climb on. A culture of adult flies is then added to the container, starting a new container culture every couple of days (to space the age of the cultures out). In a few days, you will see maggots growing in the media of the oldest containers. When those pupate

White-spotted assassin bug feeding on a wax worm, a common feeder insect that you can buy at pet stores.

and then emerge as flies, they can be shaken out into your cages to feed your pet insects. When a container has finished producing adult flies, clean it out thoroughly, set it up with fresh media, add some adult flies from an existing culture, and start the process all over again.

Earthworms

Although not a staple in the diet of many terrestrial arthropods, they serve as a convenient source of live food for those animals that will eat them. Earthworms can be raised easily in special earthworm farms, but they are so widely available and so inexpensive that most people just buy them as needed from their local bait shop. (Some pets stores carry them, too.) They keep for weeks in the refrigerator;

simply rinse them off with tap water before feeding.

Prepared Foods and Supplements

Certainly in terms of convenience, prepared foods and supplements are the easiest to use. For some animals, however, there may be an acceptance problem—the food simply does not resemble their natural diet closely enough to start up their feeding response. Carnivorous insects are the least likely to accept prepared foods because most of these species require that their food show some movement. Omnivores, herbivores, and scavengers more readily adapt to eating prepared foods.

Some commonly used prepared foods include dog kibble, dry cat food, and tropical fish flake foods. Never try to switch an animal too quickly from its normal diet to a prepared food diet. Most animals require some period of adaptation in which both their original diet and the prepared diet are fed simultaneously, while the proportion of original diet is gradually reduced over time until the switchover has been achieved.

Tropical fish flake food is an excellent supplement to the diets of many insects. It can be ground up and a little of it sprinkled onto the surface of other foods to enhance the diet in terms of protein and vitamins. There are even herbivorous tropical fish flake foods available that can be used for those insect species that cannot handle higher levels of animal protein. Be aware that these dry flakes will absorb moisture from other foods, drying them out. Adding a little water can correct this but also may allow for the formation of mold if the food is not changed out on a regular (usually daily) basis.

Food additives such as vitamin and mineral premixes are commercially available. Along the lines of the old adage "You are what you eat," some people feed these additives to their crickets or mealworms. It is thought that these "gut-loaded" prey animals will then take those added nutrients into the predator animal when they are fed to it. Reptile and amphibian hobbyists rely extensively on this technique, and it may have some application for pet insect hobbyists as well.

Water

Insects differ in their need to drink water. As mentioned, many carnivorous insects gain their needed moisture from their prey. Likewise, many plant-

African giant millipedes eating a mix of iguana food pellets and fresh vegetables.

eating bugs do the same. The moisture requirements also may vary depending on the humidity of the animal's enclosure. A humidity-loving insect kept in a xeric (dry) cage is going to need a supplemental water source. In offering water to bugs, think of how they might normally access water in the wild. Most will drink dew from plant leaves; few will drink directly from standing water like mammals do. In fact, many bugs seem unable to adapt to drinking from a standing water source and may actually tumble in and possibly drown.

To offer bugs a water source, it is usually best to cut a small piece of synthetic sponge to fit inside a shallow glass or plastic dish. Soaking the sponge with water is all that is needed to offer moisture without having standing water in the dish. Remember that these damp sponges quickly become a site where mold or fungus grow, so they need to be changed out every few days.

In other cases, moisture can be supplied to insects by way of a misting device sprayed onto decorations in the cage every day or two. This also helps to raise the humidity of the enclosure. In most cases, bottled spring water is the best source of water to use in dishes. Many people find that distilled water is best to use for misting because it does not have any dissolved minerals in it—those dissolved minerals might leave white calcium water spots on the glass or on clear portions of the cage.

Dietary Preferences of Common Bugs

is a checklist of appropriate foods for various arthropods. The following codes are us
lify the information:

G: Herbivore of leafy greens
F: Herbivore of fruit
N: Herbivore of nectar
V: Herbivore of vegetables

OM: Omnivore (feeds on a variety of
    nonliving animals and plant materi
PV: Vertebrate predator
PI: Invertebrate predator
SC: Scavenger (feeds on dead or dying
    plants and animals)

n more than one code is listed, the first one listed is the most common food for that
of animal, followed by the second most common one, and so on. If the code is followe
lowercase "j," that means that the food item is accepted by the juvenile or larval stag
ember, there can be a huge variation in the diets of animals, even those belonging to
e group. Specific dietary information is listed in the species instructions later in this

Common name	Scientific group	Code
Ants	Formicidae	OM, HN, PI, SC
Assassin bugs	Reduviidae	PI, PV
Beetles	Coleoptera	HF, HV, HN, SCj
Butterflies	Lepidoptera	HN, HF, HGj
Cave cricket	Rhaphidophoridae	OM, SC
Centipedes	Scolopendrida	PI, PV
Cockroaches	Blattodea	OM, HF, HV, SC
Crickets	Gryllidae	HV, HF, HG, OM
Grasshoppers	Acrididae	HG, HF, HV
Harvestmen	Opiliones	PI, OM, SC
Katydids	Tettigoniidae	HG, HF
Leaf insects	*Phyllium* sp	HG
Millipedes	Diplopoda	HG, HF, HV, OM, SC
Praying mantises	Mantodea	PI
Scorpions	Scorpiones	PI, PV
Spiders	Araneae	PI
Stick insects	Phasmatodea	HG
Tarantulas	Theraphosidae	PI, PV
Water bugs	Belostomatidae	PI, PV
Whip scorpions	Uropygi	PI

Chapter 4

Long-Legged Bugs

This chapter describes the care requirements for a variety of bugs that are all fairly closely related and all of which happen to have very long legs. Every one of these are true insects, but their care requirements can be very different, depending on which species of insect you have. Remember, the long legs of all of these insects can be broken easily, so always be careful when handling them.

Grasshoppers are found all over the world. This pictured grasshopper was photographed in New Mexico

Grasshoppers, Katydids, and Crickets

Grasshoppers and their kin belong to the insect order Orthoptera. There are about 20,000 different species found throughout the world. Most species can fly, and they have toughened forewings that fold to protect the larger hind wings that are used for flight. All species have chewing mouthparts used to feed on plant material. Most species also have well-developed hind legs that are used for jumping.

All Orthopterans exhibit incomplete metamorphoses as they grow, with the juveniles resembling the adult form but just having shorter wings. Although there are exceptions, crickets are ground dwellers or even burrow in

the soil. Katydids are usually found in vegetation and often have colors and shapes that match the leaves of plants. Grasshoppers, as their name suggests, usually live on grasses and hop away to avoid predators.

US Species

The easiest way to acquire Orthopterans is to collect your own. In many parts of the world, these are seasonal insects, so there may only be certain times of the year when a particular species is available. While culturing these insects is not impossible, it may be difficult to overcome this seasonal nature—even in captivity. This means that the culture may show the same cycle as their wild counterparts—very common at some times of the year and absent (or as resting eggs) at other times. The easiest way to capture larger grasshoppers is to walk along the edge of a field or other open grassy area and watch for one to take flight. Observe where it lands, walk quietly in that direction, and then quickly cover it with an insect net. Catching crickets is similar, and katydids often can be gently picked out of a bush by hand.

Eastern Lubber Grasshopper

Romalea microptera

Range: Eastern United States: North Carolina south to Florida and west to Tennessee.

Habitat: Weedy fields, along roads.

Adult Size: Up to 3 inches (7.5 cm) long.

Diet: In the wild, feeds on many different types of soft (herbaceous) plants. In captivity, feeds on well-washed romaine lettuce, rolled oats, green beans, yams, and carrots.

Housing: Large terrarium with many climbing branches.

Environment: Moderately humid and warm, above 70°F (21°C).

Dangers: Spines on hind legs can pierce skin; they also can release pungent chemicals from their mouth and thorax.

Eastern lubber grasshoppers are the largest members of the grasshopper family found in the United States. Although adults have wings, they cannot fly. Their striking coloration is a warning to predators that they are poisonous to eat. This warning—known as aposematic coloration—is common to many types of insects. The

Lubber grasshoppers can be found throughout much of the southeastern US. They are easy to care for.

most common example are wasps and bees that advertise their ability to sting with bright yellow and black colors.

After mating, the female lubber deposits an egg mass in the soil. This is surrounded by a foam that cushions the eggs and keeps them from drying out. In the wild, the eggs typically overwinter and hatch about eight months after they are deposited. In captivity, they sometimes will hatch out sooner. However, understand that adult lubbers may only live four or five months, which means that there may be times where you do not have any adult grasshoppers, only incubating eggs.

People interested in rearing large numbers of lubbers report that it helps to supply the females with cups filled with moist sand in which to lay their eggs. These cups can then be removed and placed in a plastic bag for incubation. Check these containers every few days for signs that the tiny eggs have begun to hatch.

Katydid
Microcentrum sp.

Range: Worldwide, especially in tropical regions.

The Expert Knows

Diapause

Diapause, or resting time, is important in the development of many insects. In some cases, as with stick insects, the resting phase takes place when the eggs spend the winter buried in soil or under leaves, not hatching until the weather warms in the spring. In other cases, such as with moths and butterflies, the diapause period is spent as pupae. In the case of temperate species, the diapause time allows an insect to survive a severely cold time of the year or when there is no food for them to eat. Tropical species also may have a diapause period that allows the insect to emerge at the correct time of year, perhaps avoiding the dry season.

Habitat: Usually in plants in many ecosystems.

Adult Size: Up to 5 inches (12.5 cm).

Diet: Most feed on vegetation, but some prey on other insects.

Housing: Large terrarium with ample climbing branches.

Environment: Temperate; humidity range must mirror place where the specimen was collected.

Dangers: None.

Katydids, also called bush-crickets and long-horned grasshoppers, get their name from the sounds some species make: "Katy-did, Katy-didn't." Most closely related to crickets, many katydids are green in color to match the leaves in which they are found. They are not regularly cultured in captivity, and like the lubber grasshopper, it is likely that many species lay eggs that overwinter and hatch in the spring. Try feeding your katydid the type of plant that you found it living on; these often end up being their preferred food source.

Cave Cricket

Pholeogryllus, Ceuthophilus, and related spp.

Range: Widespread in warmer regions.

Habitat: In caves and basements and under rocks and logs.

Adult Size: Up to 1.5 inches (3.8 cm), not including their long antennae and hind legs.

Diet: Scavengers. Feed on plant material and canned dog food.

Housing: Dimly lit cage with cork bark to hide under.

Environment: Warm, high humidity.

Dangers: None.

Cave crickets, also called camel crickets, have extremely long antennae and legs, making them look almost like spiders. The long antennae are used to find their way around the dark habitats in which they live. They are most commonly found in caves or in damp basements and crawl spaces of man-made structures.

Because they have poor eyesight, they can easily be captured in a net.

When in doubt, feed your katydid the same species of plant you found it on.

You can often find cave crickets in basements, crawl spaces, and old sheds.

Another way to catch them is to place some bait (canned dog food) in the bottom of a smooth plastic bucket. Leave that in an area where you have seen cave crickets; then, after a few days, come back and check the trap. Cave crickets are relatively long lived, and if their cage contains a layer of soil or sand, will even reproduce in captivity.

Because they prefer dark areas, cave crickets do not make the best display animals. One way to keep them visible is to prop a flat piece of wood or cork bark up against the front of their cage and then gently light the cage behind that. The crickets will congregate in the dark shade beneath the piece of wood but will be close to the front glass of the cage, where you can more easily observe them.

Cricket

Acheta domesticus, Gryllus sp. and related species

Range: Worldwide.

Habitat: Usually under vegetation; some burrow in soil.

Adult Size: One half to 2 inches (1.3 to 5 cm).

Diet: Most species feed on fruits, vegetables, and cereal soaked in water.

Housing: Typical terrarium with damp sand for the females to lay eggs in.

Environment: Room temperature, normal humidity.

Dangers: None.

Most often kept as a source of live food for insectivorous pets, some people keep crickets themselves as pets. Ornate cages are often used to house them. In China, a singing cricket in a cage inside the home is considered good luck. A chirping male cricket can be used to estimate the air temperature. Just count the number of chirps it makes during a 15-second period. Then, add 40 to the number of chirps. This gives a rough idea of the temperature where the animal is, in degrees Fahrenheit.

Exotic Species

There are many interesting and colorful grasshoppers found throughout the world. The painted locust (*Schistocerca melanocera*) from the Galapagos Islands is a very strong flyer and is sometimes mistaken for a small bird as it flies by. Because this group of insects has such a high potential to become major plant pests, it is unwise to move specimens from one region of the world to another. Should an escape occur, the lack of natural predators may allow these exotic insects to reproduce to huge numbers, potentially harming commercial crops. For that reason, the USDA Animal Plant Health Inspection Service rarely grants permits to import exotic grasshoppers into the United States. For people living in countries that do not restrict the importation of exotic insects, the risk of causing a problem is still so great that it is best to simply avoid keeping exotic Orthopterans as pets.

Stick and Leaf Insects

There are more than 2,400 species of stick and leaf insects in the order Phasmatodea. Collectively known as *phasmids*, they are perhaps the most

Closeup of the face of a giant prickly stick insect, showing a great resemblance to its relatives, the mantids.

Life as a Stick

Even if stick insects are not available in your area as pets, you can learn about them in books and on the Internet. One thing you will soon learn is that phasmids are masters of mimicry. The adults all look like the twigs, leaves, or branches of the plants that they feed on, so predatory reptiles and birds have a difficult time finding them. The leaf insect takes this mimicry to the highest level; their flat green bodies have veins just like plant leaves, and the edges are even brown and notched, like something has been chewing on them. Some stick insects enhance their mimicry by holding still when threatened, but a few will actually begin to rock back and forth, trying very hard to replicate a bit of twig or leaf swaying in the breeze. Even phasmid eggs look like tiny, tough plant seeds—something few animals would try to eat.

bizarre pet insects available. Related to the predatory praying mantis, all stick insects are herbivorous, and many species will only feed on certain types of plant material, choosing to starve rather than to switch to another food.

A dozen or so species are regularly cultured in captivity. However, the United States has strict laws regarding the importation and keeping of live exotic stick insects. (See Chapter 1.) There may be state and local laws regulating phasmids as well, so always check before purchasing one. Remember, just because you find stick insects for sale (especially through the Internet) does not mean that you can legally keep them. The reason that these laws are in place is that in the past, some exotic phasmids have escaped and have developed successful populations in regions of the world where they are not native. Because some of these insects are considered plant pests in their native countries, the fear is that they may harm crops in other countries as well.

In captivity, most phasmids feed on plants that are members of the rose family, collectively known as *bramble*. Some North American native species prefer to feed on oak, while some Australian types feed on eucalyptus leaves. Place freshly cut food plants in a container of water to keep them crisp and green inside the terrarium. Replace the food plants at least every three days.

In northern climates, the greatest obstacle to keeping phasmids is locating a year-round supply of food.

An alternative food for many species is firethorn, *Pyracantha*, which grows as an evergreen plant in many locations around the world. Remember that greenhouse plants have often been exposed to systemic insecticides, and these frequently will prove fatal to stick insects if those plants are used as food.

Housing stick insects is relatively easy, but the large size of some species means that the cage must be proportionally larger. In addition, baby stick insects are masters of escape, so the terrarium used to raise them must have a tight-fitting lid. While a simple screened cage will contain stick insects, it will not allow for easy temperature and humidity control. For that reason, most people rely on glass aquariums to house their stick insects. The problem with this idea is that aquariums typically are built low and long, while stick insects, due to their climbing nature, require a tall cage. The solution is to use the aquarium but stand it on its end so that it is taller. A typical screen aquarium top can be used as a "door" for the cage. If humidity levels need to be raised, the screen top can be partially or completely draped with clear plastic sheeting that will help to hold water vapor in. Then, misting with distilled water (to avoid water spots on the glass) will keep the humidity as high as the animals require.

The jungle nymph is a popular species of stick insect, although it will kick with its spiny legs.

Annam Stick Insect

Medauroidea extradentata (previously known as *Baculum extradentatum*)

Range: Vietnam.

Habitat: Shrubs.

Adult Size: 4 inches (10 cm).

Diet: Bramble, but can be adapted to a variety of plants, including romaine lettuce.

Housing: Simple small terrarium, adults and juveniles together.

Environment: Room temperature, normal humidity.

Dangers: Never allow this species to be released to the wild.

This is a very hardy species of phasmid. They seem tolerant of cooler temperatures and normal indoor humidity is fine for them. Eggs do not need to be removed for incubation and can simply be allowed to hatch in the same cage that the parents are living in. This hardiness, combined with the fact that they can reproduce by parthenogenesis (females producing young without males present), means that they could potentially grow well in many regions of the world should even one escape from captivity. Because of this, only experts should keep them, people who are certain of their ability to prevent the insects' escape to the wild. In northern climates, where the ambient winter temperature remains below freezing for long periods, this species cannot survive, so the risk is negligible.

Giant Prickly Stick Insect (Macleay's Spectre)

Extatosoma tiaratum

Range: Queensland, Australia.

Habitat: Forests.

Adult Size: 4.7 inches (12 cm).

Diet: Bramble, eucalyptus, oak.

Housing: Medium-sized terrarium with branches for climbing.

Environment: Warm but less humid than most other tropical phasmids.

Dangers: Sharp leg spines.

It has been reported that in the wild, when there is a large number of females in one location, the dropping of their eggs through the leaves of the trees they inhabit can sound like the pitter-patter of raindrops. In captive culture for many years, reports from Great Britain indicate that some of these long-term populations have begun to fail. This may be due to constant inbreeding; when populations were previously mixed among hobbyists, the mortality problem seemed to lessen.

Tiny Mantis?

Occasionally, when collecting new insects, you may come across what you think is a baby mantis. Look closely. If it does not have a thickened forewing covering the more delicate hind wing, you may have found a relatively rare insect known as a mantidfly.

Giant Spiny Stick Insect

Eurycantha calcarata

Range: Indonesia, Papua New Guinea.

Habitat: Rainforest, in trees and shrubs.

Adult Size: 6 inches (15 cm).

Diet: Bramble, oak, and possibly ivy.

Housing: Longer (than tall) terrarium; may spend time on floor of cage.

Environment: 80°F (26.5°C) and 70% or higher relative humidity.

Dangers: Sharp leg spines.

This nocturnal species often hides under leaf litter or bark during the day, coming out at night to feed on leaves. Heavy bodied, dingy brown in color, with relatively short legs, this species is not very attractive as far as phasmids go. Giant spiny stick insects will try to pinch your hand with their leg spines when handled, although reports are that with time, they will eventually become accustomed to routine handling.

Jungle Nymph

Heteropteryx dilatata

Range: Western Malaysia.

Habitat: Rainforest, in trees and shrubs.

Adult Size: At least 6.5 inches (17 cm).

Diet: Bramble, guava, possibly ivy, oak, and hawthorn.

Housing: Large terrarium with many climbing spots.

Environment: Warm and humid, 80°F (26.5°C) and 70% or higher humidity.

Dangers: Sharp spines on body.

This is a very popular species. The bright green females are probably the

Unfortunately, the fascinating leaf insects are delicate and hard to keep.

heaviest (but not the longest) of all species of phasmid. The brown-colored males can fly, and females are prone to kicking with their legs and using their sharp spines to drive away predators (and people). Females lay their eggs in soil, so the cage bottom should be covered with dry silica sand. Sift it to remove the eggs; the eggs must then be incubated in damp sand for up to 18 months before they hatch.

Leaf Insect

Phyllium giganteum and related spp.

Range: Southeast Asia.

Habitat: Rainforest, in shrubs.

Adult Size: Females of some species up to 4 inches (10 cm).

Diet: Bramble, oak.

Housing: Medium-sized terrarium.

Environment: Warm, with high humidity: 82°F (28°C) and 60% humidity.

Dangers: None.

Perhaps the most sought-after members of the phasmids, leaf insects truly look just like leaves, down to little brown "fungus spots" and "leaf veins." Many leaf insects seem to be parthenogenic, meaning that females can produce viable eggs in the absence of any male to fertilize them. This can make propagation easier because you do not need to be concerned with matching up males and females at the right times. On the other hand, colonies of leaf insects often die out over time; this may be due in part to the lack of genetic diversity. Because they are prone to difficulties when shedding their exoskeletons, you must mist this

You can find northern walkingsticks from southeastern Canada to the Mid-Atlantic and Mid-Western states.

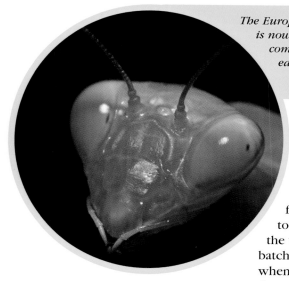

The European mantis is now fairly common in the eastern US.

maintained as a colony, just like the tropical species. The main difficulty is feeding the colony during the winter, when there are no leaves on the trees. In the wild, the adult insects die off during the colder months, and their eggs spend the winter buried in the leaf litter on the forest floor. Some hobbyists opt to close down their colony during the winter by simply refrigerating a batch of eggs to hatch out in the spring when the leaves have returned to the trees.

For those who want to try to keep their colony going all winter, there are a few tricks that can be tried. First, keep the population of the walkingsticks as low as possible so that there are fewer animals that need to be fed. Then, before the leaves change color in the fall, try freezing a number of oak leaves in water. (Leaves that are frozen in air will turn soft and mushy, and the walkingsticks won't eat them.) These leafsicles can be thawed out as needed during the winter. Finally, try feeding the insects *Pyracantha* (an evergreen shrub), or contact a greenhouse to see if they have specimens of a plant related to the oak family that the insects might eat. Still, despite these efforts, it is very common to lose a colony of walkingsticks during the winter.

species daily with distilled water to help to keep their cuticle (skin) moist.

Northern Walkingstick

Diapheromera fermorata

Range: North America.

Habitat: Oak forests.

Adult Size: 3.5 inches (9 cm).

Diet: Oak, cherry, and locust leaves.

Housing: Small terrarium; will spend most of the time on the food plants.

Environment: Mist daily; room temperature is fine.

Dangers: None.

For insect hobbyists in the northern United States, this species is really the only type of stick insect they will legally have available to them. Still, they are an interesting species and can be

Long-Legged Bugs

Mantis Defense Tactics

Some species of mantids have special ways to keep other animals from eating them. The Chinese mantis will attempt to strike out and pinch predators with its front legs. Some mantids have bright-colored spots on the inside of these legs. When attacked, they spread their front legs, flashing the spots. This is supposed to startle attacking birds. In some species, this technique is combined with spreading of their wings—truly an amazing sight!

Queensland Titan (Wuelfing's Stick Insect)

Acrophylla wuelfingi

Range: Queensland, Australia.

Habitat: Forests.

Adult Size: 8.5 inches (22 cm).

Diet: Eucalyptus in the wild, bramble in captivity.

Housing: Large cage with ample branching.

Environment: Warm, moderate humidity.

Dangers: None.

The adult females of this species may live for almost a year. Their eggs may take four to five months to hatch, and the young take about the same amount of time to reach maturity. Males can fly, while the females are too heavy to do so. This species is the longest phasmid that is routinely kept in captivity.

Mantises are efficient and voracious predators.

Praying Mantises

Praying mantises are very popular pet insects for many people. Collectively known as mantids, there are about 2,000 species of this group of insects found throughout the world. All feed on live prey animals (usually insect species but sometimes feeding on small amphibians and lizards). The common name praying mantis comes from the way many species hold their front legs up, as if in prayer. Some people refer to them incorrectly as "preying mantises," but this is actually fairly descriptive, since all species are predators. The word *mantis* is apparently based on the Greek word *mantes*, which means fortune teller, again a reference to the way these insects hold their front legs.

Female mantids lay their eggs in a foamy mass called an ootheca.

The foamy covering to this egg mass serves to protect the incubating eggs from the ravages of weather, as well as some predators. Once hatched, the baby mantids go through incomplete metamorphoses in a series of molts until they reach adult size.

Mantids are excellent predators—they have great eyesight and even have binocular vision that helps them gauge the distance of their prey to more effectively capture them with their raptorial (front) legs. In captivity, most mantids will feed readily on live crickets, although some of the smaller species may require tiny prey items such as wingless fruit flies (especially when the mantids first hatch out). House mantids singly, so they don't eat each other.

Egg case (ootheca) of a praying mantis. You may find these attached to shrubs in your yard.

Mantids are well known for being cannibalistic, and the story of the female mantid biting off the head of the male during mating is sometimes true in captivity. Males of most species are a bit smaller and have longer antennae and longer wings. To try to avoid the male being killed by the female, wait for three weeks after the male and female mantids have gone through their terminal (final sixth or seventh) molt. Feed them both very well for the last week, and then introduce them to the same cage. It often helps to give the female mantis a cricket to eat right before the male is added to her cage. Mating will usually follow within an hour or two, and then you can remove the male (if still alive).

The female will then begin producing ootheca, and up to a dozen may be produced from a single mating. Juvenile mantids will also prey on

Mantis Myth

There is an urban legend that it is illegal to kill praying mantises in the United States, a crime that carries a fine. Although not true, there is certainly no reason to kill mantids—they often prove to be beneficial insects.

one another, but this can sometimes be used to an advantage. Often, more than one ootheca will hatch, resulting in far too many baby mantids for the hobbyist to easily raise. By simply allowing some of the young to feed on one another (as cruel as this sounds), you can not only supply the remaining mantids with a ready source of live food but also reduce the total number of mantids you are raising at the same time. Then, when the number

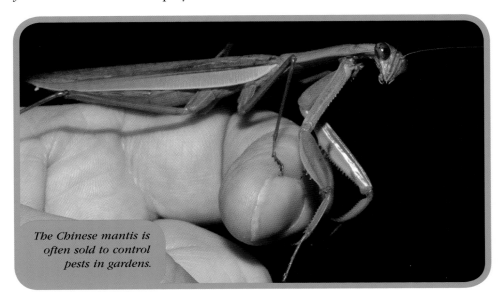

The Chinese mantis is often sold to control pests in gardens.

of baby mantids has reached a more manageable number, you can move each one to a small pill bottle or other container and raise it in isolation.

Species Found in the United States

European Mantis
Mantis religiosa

Range: Europe, introduced elsewhere (including eastern United States).

Habitat: Usually meadows, on plants.

Adult Size: 2.8 inches (7 cm).

Diet: Live insects.

Housing: Small terrarium with branches for climbing.

Environment: Room temperature, normal humidity.

Dangers: None.

The species name refers to "religious" or "pious," again in reference to the praying stance taken by these insects in the way they hold their front legs. They were introduced into the United States around 1900. Although relatively common in the eastern portions of the country, ranging north to Canada, they are never found in large numbers, and due to their cannibalistic nature, are always found singly. The female lays an ootheca on a plant stem, and this incubates over the winter with the baby mantids hatching out in the spring. Like all mantids, they can become relatively tame and seem to learn that people bring them food in captivity.

Tropical Mantids Sometimes Kept as Pets

- flower mantis (*Creobroter* sp.), southern India
- dead leaf mantis (*Deroplatys desiccate*), Southeast Asia
- Indian rose mantis (*Gongylus gongylodes*), southern India, Sri Lanka
- giant Indian mantis (*Hierodula grandis*), India
- orchid mantis (*Hymenopus coronatus*) Malaysia, Indonesia
- ghost mantis (*Phyllocrania paradoxa*), Madagascar
- African mantis (*Sphodromantis lineola*), Tanzania
- elegant mantis (*Theopropus elegans*), Malaysia

Chinese Mantis
Tenodera aridifolia (sinensis)

Range: China, introduced into the eastern United States.

Habitat: Meadows and gardens.

Adult Size: Reported to 6 inches

Long-Legged Bugs

(15 cm), but most are 4 inches (10 cm) or less.

Diet: Live insects, even reported to eat hummingbirds!

Housing: Small terrarium with branches for climbing.

Environment: Room temperature, mist daily.

Dangers: None.

This species is widely found throughout the United States, possibly because the oothecae are often sold to help to reduce plant and garden pests. Called IPM (Integrated Pest Management), this is the technique of using fewer chemicals and more natural environmental resources to control plant pests. Males are typically green, and the females are brownish. Some people report that the eye color of some mantids can change throughout the day, from clear to black at night. However, it is unclear if this is an actual color change or just the eye's reflection changing under different conditions.

Carolina Mantis

Stagmomantis carolina

Range: Southeastern United States north to Indiana.

Habitat: Meadows and woodlands.

Adult Size: 3 inches (7.5 cm).

Diet: Live insects.

Can you spot the mantis? A master of disguise, the orchid mantis waits for food to come to it.

Housing: Small terrarium with branches for climbing.

Environment: Room temperature, normal humidity.

Dangers: None.

Usually colored a mottled grayish brown, this mantid is the state insect of South Carolina. There is some concern that the two introduced species of mantids may be outcompeting the Carolina mantis, especially in the northern portions of its range.

Exotic species

The care for most species of exotic mantids is similar to native species, except that all of these are tropical, so their oothecae should not be exposed to a cold (diapause) stage. These species need to be kept in warm, humid conditions; 82°F (28°C) and 60 percent humidity are usually appropriate. Many of these creatures are among the most fantastic of all insects. Some resemble tiny orchids; others look just like dead dried leaves. Hobbyists have been attracted to these tropical mantids for years, but recently, in the United States, the department of agriculture (USDA-APHIS) has made the determination that exotic mantids fall into the class of restricted "plant pests."

As with populations of some terrestrial arthropods, it seems that with many of these mantids, it is difficult to propagate them beyond the first two generations. There is typically no difficulty in getting a wild pair to lay fertile eggs, but their offspring often do not reproduce well. Some people attribute this to genetic inbreeding, although it is difficult to see how this could occur in just one generation. More likely, there is some unknown environmental need that is lacking in the care we give these creatures.

FAMILY-FRIENDLY TIP

Raising Praying Mantises

Female mantises lay eggs in a mass called an ootheca. This brown papery material protects the delicate eggs during the winter so that they can hatch in the spring. You can buy mantis oothecae from biological supply houses as well as from companies that supply biological control animals for gardens. It can be a fun and engaging project for you and your children to raise some baby mantises for later release in your garden.

As mentioned in this chapter, baby mantises will prey upon one another—something that is difficult to explain to small children. Because hundreds of baby mantises may emerge from a single ootheca, it is usually best to have the children release most of them in your garden and keep just a few in pill jars and feed them on fruit flies as previously described. Remember, mantises are seasonal insects, so if you want to try this project with your children, schedule the ootheca to arrive in the spring so that the mantises you release can find insects in the garden on which to feed.

Long-Legged Bugs

Chapter 5

Bugs That

Scurry, Swim, and Fly

This chapter gives care information for pet bugs that can crawl, go underwater, or even fly. Most are smaller species, and all have relatively short legs. Most are also true insects but their care requirements still can be very different. Just remember that although these species are in the same chapter of this book, they may need different care.

Cockroaches

The 4,000 or so species of cockroaches are found in tropical and temperate regions of the world. Only about 30 of these species have adapted to living in the warm homes of humans, where they are considered household pests. Most species are nocturnal and prefer the safety of confining, tight spaces (meaning they are what is known as positively thigmotaxic). Females produce eggs inside an ootheca (egg case), and the eggs go through incomplete metamorphoses as the young cockroaches mature. Most cockroaches are scavengers, eating all types of dead or decaying organic material.

Even the most enthusiastic insect hobbyist may question the idea of keeping cockroaches as pets. However, one species, the Madagascar hissing cockroach, is a popular classroom animal and makes a suitable pet insect because it will not live as a pest inside homes if it happens to escape. In the United States, the legality of owning these exotic cockroaches is not clear. The United States Department of Agriculture Animal Plant Health Inspection Service (USDA APHIS) considers many of the species to be plant pests, yet they are frequently offered for sale by pet stores and even scientific supply houses. Independently, some states also regulate the sale of cockroaches, so it pays to ask the proper agencies before purchasing pet cockroaches from outside your own state.

Knowing that the pest species of cockroach can cause disease problems

Madagascar hissing roaches are interesting and popular pets sold in many pet stores.

One good thing about hissing roaches is that they will eat almost anything. Feed yours fruits, vegetables, and dog or cat kibble.

in humans, many people fear that the same problem may occur with pet cockroaches. This fear is unfounded. Pest roaches carry disease organisms from the sewers and other unclean areas where they live into human areas on their feet. Unless you don't clean your cockroaches' cage and then let them walk across your food, there is really no danger of disease from keeping them as pets. Cockroaches themselves are relatively disease free. As long as they are kept under proper environmental conditions, they will do very well. Sometimes, mites are seen crawling along the bodies of larger cockroaches. These are not parasites and will not infest your home or cause any other problems, so they can just be ignored.

Because most cockroaches are kept in cages containing many individuals as a breeding colony, one problem soon becomes clear. Many species of cockroach are very fast, and a few can fly. At some point, the cage they are being kept in will become soiled with their waste and may begin to smell. How do you clean a cage full of cockroaches, their eggs, and their babies? The easiest way is to set up an entirely new second cage and move as many of the adults, nymphs, and oothecae over to it as you can. Then, as cruel as it sounds, put the old cage in a freezer, killing the few extra roaches that you could not catch. Next, clean out the old cage and get it ready for the next "cage swap." Fortunately, this needs to be done only once every six months to a year.

Common Species

Madagascar Hissing Cockroach
Gromphadorhina portentosa

Range: Madagascar.

Habitat: Under fallen leaves and logs in the forests of Madagascar.

Adult Size: 3.75 inches (9.5 cm), but most only reach 2.75 inches (7 cm).

Diet: Vegetables, fruit, dried cat food.

Housing: Dark cage with cork bark to hide under.

Environment: Warm and moist, 85°F (29°C) and 50% humidity.

Dangers: Harmless, but their warning hiss may startle some people.

This species is by far the best pet species of cockroach. They feed well on a variety of foods, and like all cockroaches, should be offered a dish of water to drink from. Because the smaller nymphs may have difficulty navigating a water dish, it is always best to cut a piece of synthetic sponge to fit inside the dish to reduce the amount of standing water present (which could drown the baby insects). Remember to replace this sponge on a regular basis to reduce odors.

As with some other species of insect that have been cultured in captivity for long periods, it seems that populations of hissing cockroaches can become inbred (too closely related to one another). This results in smaller animals and less active reproduction. If you notice this, try introducing some new animals from a different colony. This often strengthens the genetics of your population and reduces the problem. However, new wild stock is rarely (if ever) imported from Madagascar, so it is likely that most specimens in captivity are already fairly closely related to one another anyway.

This species is considered *ovoviviparous*, a term that refers to animals that produce eggs that hatch inside the female and the young appear to be born alive. This species is really the only one of the group that is large and slow enough to be easily handled outside of their cage.

The giant cockroach has an impressive size, but its speed and flying ability make it hard to handle.

You will need a secure cage to house *Cuban green roaches*; they are excellent escape artists.

Giant Cockroach

Blaberus giganteus

Range: Central and South America.

Habitat: Caves.

Adult Size: 3.5 inches (9 cm).

Diet: Vegetables, dried cat or dog food, some fruit.

Housing: Dark cage with vertical climbing surfaces.

Environment: Warm and humid, 85°F (29°C) at about 40% humidity.

Dangers: None.

Giant cockroaches are fairly easy to raise, although some colonies have difficulty "taking off" at first. Some people believe that this is due to males killing one another when kept in low numbers. In higher densities, the fighting seems to diminish. Once established, colonies can live for years. For this and other species that prefer high temperatures and moderate humidity, it often works well to use a reptile cage heating pad beneath the cage. This warms the soil (and the air above it) without drying it out too much like suspending a lightbulb over the cage will do. Additionally, the use of heat lamps should be avoided with cockroaches because many species are nocturnal and shun light.

Cuban Green Cockroach

Panchlora nivea

Range: Cuba and southern US.

Habitat: Under leaf litter or pieces of rotted wood.

Adult Size: 1 inch (2.5 cm).

Diet: Fruit, vegetables, and flake fish food.

There are more species of beetles than of any other type of insect. This is a scarab beetle on a lilac flower.

Housing: Small containers with close-fitting lids.

Environment: Warm and humid.

Dangers: None.

This dainty colorful cockroach does not bring to mind the typical "pest" cockroach for many people, so they may be received by other members of the household more readily than other typical roaches. Able to fly, the Cuban green is also an expert escape artist, so keeping them in their container can be a real challenge. Some people resort to double containing species like this that can escape so readily. Placing one container inside another also makes it easier when it comes time to clean or service the cage. Some hobbyists place the cage inside a refrigerator for a short time to slow down their pet insects.

This is not recommended because the temperature difference between simply slowing down your pets and actually freezing them is often very small.

"Pest" Species

Few people have an interest in keeping the typical pest species of cockroaches as pets, but some people do maintain colonies of the large American cockroach *Periplaneta americana* for use as a food source for their other pets, including tarantulas and lizards. Colonies of this species produce a strong odor if not cleaned often enough. The Surinam cockroach *Pycnoscelis surinamensis* is sometimes available but spends most of its time buried under the soil, so it does not make a good pet species. Only insect researchers (such as those working on new insecticides) would want to raise German cockroaches because they are such a pest in people's homes.

Other Species

False Death's Head Roach, Blaberus discoidalis

Often incorrectly identified but commonly sold in the pet trade, this smaller species does not have a "death's head" mark on its pronotum (the top covering of the first segment of an insect's thorax). Adults can live for over a year in captivity and reach a length of 1.75 inches (4.5 cm).

Lobster Roach, Nauphoeta cinerea

Lobster roaches are commonly used as a food source for pet reptiles because they are softer bodied than many other insects. They also lack the ability to release an offensive odor as so many other types of cockroach can.

Pale-Bordered Field Cockroach, Pseudomops septentrionalis

A colorful, very small species from the southern United States that only reaches 5/8 of an inch (1.5 cm) in length. Colonies can be fed on dry cat food. They should be offered some twigs and branches to climb on.

True Death's Head Roach, Blaberus craniifer

Adults of this species have the signature "death's head" mark on their pronotum. Both adults and nymphs are darker than other members of this genus.

Zebra Roach, Eurycotis decipiens

This boldly patterned species originates from Central America and can reach a length of 1.25 inches (3.2 cm). Although they cannot fly, they are very fast and capable of escaping most terrariums, especially when the lid is removed to service the container. They also can release a chemical that has an odor that some people find offensive.

Beetles

About one-third of all species of insect alive today are a member of the beetle order Coleoptera. Beetles have evolved to live in many different habitats, including underwater. There are tiny beetles—the size of the head of a pin—and monster species up to 7 inches (18 cm) long. Although they vary in size, shape, and color, they all have one common feature: Known as *elytra*, all beetles have hardened forewings that cover the membranous wings beneath them. All beetles undergo complete metamorphosis: egg, larva, pupa, adult. Most beetles are herbivores or scavengers, while a few are predatory.

Many beetles are important to humans. Some are plant pests that feed on farmers' crops, while others, like ladybugs, feed on plant pests and are considered beneficial insects.

Because of their wide variation, the care requirements for beetles in captivity varies. Some are easy to keep, like mealworm beetles, while others

are considered virtually impossible, like fireflies or lightning bugs. Many beetle species have specific food requirements, and these requirements often change between the larval and adult stages. In addition, the pupa stage of many beetles is very lengthy, making it difficult to maintain an active colony. In some giant beetles, a colony may only consist of animals in the pupa or larva stage for two or three years before new adults emerge.

Because their care is so different, aquatic beetles are discussed later, in the section covering aquatic insects.

Common Species

Darkling Beetle

Tenebrio sp.

Range: Worldwide.

Habitat: Varied, but often dry areas.

Adult Size: Up to around 1.2 inches (3 cm).

Mealworms, a common food item for pet reptiles and tarantulas, are the larvae of a species of darkling beetle.

Diet: Plant material, including various grains.

Housing: Simple screened cage.

Environment: Normal household conditions for most species.

Dangers: None.

There are perhaps 15,000 species of darkling beetle belonging to the family Tenebrionidae. Most are dark colored, generalized beetles. Some species (such as the mealworm) are very easily kept, and some are used as foods for other animals. (See Chapter 2.) Most darkling beetles can be colony raised by keeping the adults in a cage with enough substrate so that the larvae can bury and form into pupae. Because most darkling beetles are generalized feeders, offering them a variety of vegetables lightly dusted with tropical fish flake food is often all they need to grow and reproduce. Some people are allergic to the shed skins of the larvae of these beetles.

Flower Beetles

Eudicella gralli, E. smithi, and others

Range: Tropical Africa.

Habitat: Forest floor.

Adult Size: 1.6 inches (4 cm).

Diet: Adults eat fruit, larva feeds on compost.

Housing: Normal aquarium with a lid.

Environment: Humid, 77°F (25°C).

Dangers: None.

Flower beetles are popular pets because they are moderately large, very colorful, and relatively easy to care for.

Desert Survival

In the Namibian Desert in Africa, a species of darkling beetle obtains its moisture by raising its body and letting the water vapor in the air condense on its body. As tiny water droplets form, they trickle down to the head of the beetle and are then absorbed through the beetle's mouth.

Because they are considered exotic species, you will need a permit to keep them in the United States. Adults can be housed as a group and fed soft-bodied fruits (such as banana or mango) dusted with tropical fish food now and then.

Males can be identified from females because they have a small branched cephalic horn emerging from their head. Females will lay their eggs in the soil of their primary container. You need to sift through this and periodically remove any larvae that you find, and transplant them to rearing containers. Plastic shoeboxes work well for this. Just mix up potting soil, crushed leaves, and decomposing wood (no pine tree material); keep it damp;

Bugs That Scurry, Swim, and Fly

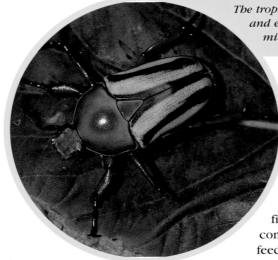

The tropical flower beetles are beautiful and easy to care for, but you need a permit to keep them in the US.

as pets in Japan, this species is difficult to raise due to its long larval stage. It can take two years for an egg from this species to eventually develop into an adult beetle (that may only live for six to eight months). Male Hercules beetles need to be isolated from one another to keep them from fighting. Development is through complete metamorphoses. The larvae feed on rotted wood. Full breeding instructions for this species are beyond the scope of this book, but information is available on the Internet.

and the larva will grow and eventually form a cocoon (nymph cells). These can be moved to a smaller container to wait for the adult beetle (imago) to emerge.

Hercules Beetle

Dynastes hercules

Range: South and Central America.

Habitat: Tropical rainforest.

Adult Size: Males can reach 6.7 inches (17 cm).

Diet: Adults eat fruit and sap; larvae feed on rotted wood.

Housing: Typical large insect cage.

Environment: Humid, 77°F (25°C).

Dangers: None.

The males of this species are considered the longest species of beetle when their huge horns are taken into consideration. Wildly popular

Because Hercules beetles are an exotic species, a permit is needed to keep them in the United States; however, there is also a smaller member of the genus found in North America that goes by a similar name, the eastern Hercules beetle (*Dynastes tityus*). Because they are native, no permit is required. Adults of this species can be fed watered-down maple syrup, while the larvae feed on composted material from deciduous trees. In addition to the 12- to 18-month-long life cycle, the females seem to require a period of hibernation before they will produce viable eggs, so this species is complicated to care for in captivity. The related Grant's rhinoceros beetle (*D. granti*) lives in the western United States and grows to a length of 3 inches (7.5 cm).

Lady Beetle

Hippodamia convergens and related species

Range: Worldwide, temperate regions.

Habitat: Fields, gardens, woods.

Adult Size: 3/8 inch (1 cm).

Diet: Preys on smaller insects.

Housing: Pickle jar as a temporary home.

Environment: Normal room conditions.

Dangers: None.

Known as lady beetles, ladybugs, or ladybirds, these insects are perhaps the most widely recognized beetle, even by small children. These beneficial insects are used as biological agents to control various plant infestations of mealybugs and aphids. However, they are specialized predators and will not easily convert to substitute foods. Therefore, if the species of lady beetle you find is one that feeds on aphids, you are going to need to collect aphids for it. It is best to keep these insects as temporary pets, observing them for a few days and then letting them go free.

The Hercules beetle is among the largest of insects. Even the larva is an enormous bug. The grubs eat rotting wood, while the adults eat tree sap—maple syrup in captivity.

Bugs That Scurry, Swim, and Fly

adults feed on plant sap.

Housing: Temporary cage.

Environment: Normal room conditions.

Dangers: May bite when handled.

The giant stag beetle may be becoming rare in its native range due to woodland development. They are also strongly attracted to lights at night, which may cause adult beetles to die prematurely. Their strong attraction to these lights can be used to capture them. Most people find stag beetles in that fashion; it is much more difficult to find them in the woods where they live. Because the adults feed on plant sap, they really can only be temporary pets and should be released after observing them for a day or two.

Other Beetles

With so many species of beetles in the world, it is impossible to list all that can be kept as pets. Remember that the same laws apply to beetles as to other exotic insects, so always check before purchasing any species of beetle that is not native to the area where you live. For many species, you will have to work out their care requirements on your own. To do this, it helps to know where the beetle was collected—the rule is that (for plant-feeding insects, at least) the plant that you find them on is often their food source. If you want to try to raise a species of beetle through all of its life stages, remember that for many beetles, the larva (grub) stage often lives in and feeds on rotting wood and plant material, and then they often pupate in the same material. The

FAMILY-FRIENDLY TIP

The Ladybug Rhyme

The nursery rhyme known to many of us as:
"Ladybug, ladybug, fly away home, Your house is on fire and your children are alone!"

Is more accurately recited as:
"Ladybug, ladybug, fly away home, Your house is on fire, your children do roam.
Except little Nan, who sits in a pan, Weaving gold laces as fast as she can."

Originally, the rhyme referred to the practice in Europe of burning fields of hop plants to reduce the aphid pests. It is thought that even the people of olden days knew that ladybugs are beneficial insects and wanted them to "fly away home" to avoid the fires that burned the fields.

Stag Beetle

Lucanus elaphus

Range: Eastern United States.

Habitat: Wooded areas.

Adult Size: 2.4 inches (6 cm).

Diet: Larvae feed on rotted wood;

table Other Beetles That Can Be Kept as Pets offers some basic care advice for some species of adult beetles that have been kept in captivity with at least some fairly good results.

Miscellaneous Bugs

With so many species available as potential pets, no book can cover every possible type of terrestrial arthropod. This section discusses the care requirements of a few types that do not fit with other groups of animals discussed in this book but that are still routinely available as pets. The species here are not necessarily less popular than those discussed in the other sections; they simply have very different care requirements.

Ants

Ants are social insects—that is, they live together as groups. There are more than 10,000 different species of ants in the world today, all belonging

There are many species of lady beetles displaying a wide range of colors and patterns.

Other Beetles That Can Be Kept as Pets

Common name	Scientific name	Adult Diet	Notes
American burying beetle	*Nicrophorus americanus*	Scavengers (carrion)	Endangered throughout much of its range, agencies are attempting to restore its populations
Caterpillar killer	*Calosoma scrutator*	Active predators that prefer caterpillars	A beneficial species that eats plant pest species
Click beetle	Elateridae family	Tree leaves?	Jumps with a "click" to avoid predators
Confused flour beetle	*Tribolium confusum*	Grains and flour	Tiny beetle, easily kept in a jar of flour, may serve as food for other animals
Dung beetle	*Canthon imatator*	Animal dung	Need a ready source of dung from a farm to feed them
Goliath beetle	*Goliathus goliatus*	Fruits (banana and melon), sugar water	Difficult to raise through entire life cycle
Grapevine beetle	*Pelidnota punctata*	Grape leaves, fruit	Adults live for only a month or two
Ground beetle	Carabidae family	Scavengers	Fast crawlers, nocturnal
Japanese beetle	*Popillia japonica*	Leaves of many plants	A common plant pest but colorful
Tiger beetle	*Cicindela* sp.	Other insects	Adults fly well, may bite when handled

to the family Formicidae. They live in colonies of a few dozen to millions of individuals. The queen ant produces eggs for the colony. These are fertilized by a few male ants (called drones) living in the group.

Most of the ants that you see moving around are either worker or soldier ants. Worker ants gather food for the colony, while soldier ants protect the colony from attack by predators or other ant colonies. They also undergo complete metamorphoses, so at any one time, a colony of ants also contains eggs, larvae, and pupae, along with the adults. Because of their complex social structure and complicated life cycle, ant colonies are difficult to maintain in captivity. The ant farms that you see for sale do not contain an ant queen, only worker ants. When the worker ants die of old age, no new ants will be born and the colony will die out after a few months. A few zoos and insectariums keep colonies of ants for exhibit, usually honeypot ants or leafcutter ants. These colonies require a lot of care and must be housed in specialized cages—more than most insect hobbyists are willing or able to give them. Some ants can bite or sting, and some can give off toxic substances.

If you want to try to keep some ants as pets, you should first find a colony (an anthill) of large black ants and then use a pooter (see Chapter 2) to collect as many workers as you can. Collect the ants close to the hill, because if you mix ants from different colonies, they will fight with one another. Once you have collected a number of the ants,

move them to a container holding sand mixed with some soil.

Because so many ant activities are below ground, it helps if you devise a way to view them there. Ant farms are very narrow, transparent containers, so any ant tunnel made is likely to be close to the viewing panel. A jar, with a can set in the center and the sand/soil mixture added around it, will also keep the ants' tunnels near enough to the glass sides of the jar so that you can see them work.

The lid on your ant container will need to have two holes in it, about 1/2 inch (1.3 cm) in diameter. These are kept plugged with cotton most of the time. To feed the ants, remove one of the cotton plugs and add a tiny amount of fruit or bread. If they don't eat that, try a small dead insect such as a cricket. The second hole is for adding moisture. The sand needs to be kept slightly damp so that the ants' tunnels will hold together. Too much water will cause the food to spoil. You should be able to keep a group of ants in a container such as this for a month or two.

Assassin Bugs

There are two species of assassin bug that are routinely available as pets: the red-spotted assassin bug (*Platymeris rhadamanthus*) and the white-spotted assassin bug (*Platymeris biguttata*). There is also a species called the "orange-spotted" assassin bug that may just be a hybrid or variety of the other two types. These insects come from Africa and reach an adult size of 1.5 inches (3.8 cm). Adults may live for up to two years.

White-spotted assassin bug. Assassin bugs deliver a painful bite, so do not handle them.

These insects belong to the group of true bugs and have the ability to bite humans. Species of this group are also called conenose, wheel bugs, and kissing bugs. In South America, the bites of assassin bugs transmit the blood parasite that causes Chagas disease in humans. More than 20,000 people die each year due to complications from this disease. While there are no reports of pet assassin bugs causing Chagas disease in their owners, many species can deliver an extremely painful bite.

In one unconfirmed case, a person was bitten by a West African *Platymeris* species and went into total cardiac arrest. Although he was revived by emergency personnel, it was by pure luck—he was discovered by a coworker as he lay unconscious on the floor. Always wear gloves if you need

to handle assassin bugs directly, or better yet, transfer them as needed by scooping them into a plastic cup with a lid.

Assassin bugs prefer less humid but warm conditions around 78°F (26°C). Their cage must be escape-proof, and the bottom must be covered with soil or a mixture of peat and sand. Pieces of cork bark serve as climbing and hiding spaces for the bugs. Assassin bugs are predatory, eating crickets and other small insects. They sometimes leave quite a bit of food uneaten, and you need to remove it from the cage to keep it from smelling bad.

Platymeris sp. are communal insects that can be kept together as groups, often as many as two dozen in a 20-gallon (75-l) container. They deposit eggs in the soil in the cage, and you can allow them to hatch as they

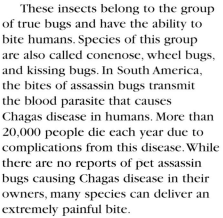

lay. The young will grow up alongside the adults, scrounging for what food they can find. The adults may feed on some of the nymphs, so move them into smaller containers for rearing if you want to maximize their survival.

Butterflies and Caterpillars

Butterflies are perhaps the most familiar example of an insect that undergoes a complete metamorphosis. Because the adults need to fly, they usually cannot be kept except in specialized greenhouses and are better off being released into their natural habitat. Still, the caterpillars can make interesting, if temporary, pets.

All caterpillars are herbivorous, but many will only feed on one or two types of plants, refusing to eat anything else. For this reason, do not attempt to keep any caterpillar unless you have a good source of its normal food plant. There are two ways to determine what plants a particular caterpillar needs to eat. One is to identify it as to what species it is, then look up that name and the species' food source in books or on the Internet. The second is to observe the caterpillar where you found it. Often, caterpillars spend almost their entire larval stage living on the host plant on which they feed. So, if you find a caterpillar on a tomato plant, you can be pretty certain that this is its normal food. If a caterpillar ends up not feeding on the plant material you offer it, please release it where you found it after a day or two.

The larvae of a few species of butterflies and moths can cause skin irritation in humans. Called *nettling*, the reaction feels very similar to that produced by contact with the stinging nettle plant. Like the new world tarantulas discussed in Chapter 6, these caterpillars possess urticating hairs (irritating hairs that can become imbedded in your skin) that cause localized reactions in humans who pick them up. One well-known species that can cause this problem is the puss caterpillar (*Megalopyge opercularis*). Because accurate field identification of the problem species is difficult, it is best to avoid handling any unknown caterpillar with your bare hands. Many of the nettling species have hair-like material called setae emerging from their bodies, and some are brightly colored as a way to advertise their nettling ability to potential predators.

Honeybees

People may be surprised to learn that the most commonly kept species of insect is the honeybee. However, most people don't keep them as pets, but rather to pollinate their crops or to gather honey from their hives. An area

FAMILY-FRIENDLY TIP

Raising Monarch Butterflies

A fascinating pastime for young and old alike is raising monarch butterflies from egg to adulthood and then releasing them into the wild. Nothing teaches children the wonders of life more than to see their pet change from a creeping caterpillar to a strange unmoving chrysalis and then into a beautiful butterfly that flies away.

The only really difficult step in this process is the first one: finding monarch eggs to raise. First, locate a field that has many milkweed plants growing in it. Then, every few days, inspect the undersides of the leaves for the presence of monarch eggs. Once you find leaves with eggs on them, break the leaves off, take them home, and place them in a container. Keep the cage clean and the plants moist by layering the bottom of the cage with damp paper towels.

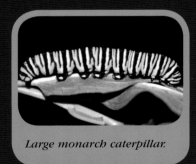

Large monarch caterpillar.

Monarch egg on a milkweed leaf.

Monarch chrysalis.

Once the eggs hatch out, the tiny caterpillars soon will begin to grow. In fact, they will grow rapidly, and you'll need to change the damp paper towels and the milkweed leaves every day or so.

Eventually, the now very large caterpillars will stop feeding and remain still. If you are observant, you may even get to see the caterpillar preparing its chrysalis. After a week or so, the bright green chrysalis will turn clear and the spotted wings of the adult butterfly may even be visible. Watch closely and you'll see the butterfly emerge. As soon as its wings have dried, release it outdoors (on a sunny day).

Clear chrysalis. You can see the butterfly inside.

A monarch just out of its chrysalis.

where beehives are kept is called an *apiary*, and a person who raises bees is called an *apiarist* or *beekeeper*. If you live in the right area, you can maintain a few hives and sell the honey and beeswax from them and have a hobby that pays you! Setting up a hive and the related equipment can be costly, however. In some states, you'll need an apiary license because there are many diseases, such as bacterial infections or mites, that can infect a hive of bees. If you have sick bees, they may fly far enough away from your hive to carry that disease to somebody else's hive, causing them serious problems. A license and site inspection are often needed to ensure that your bees are healthy. For more information, consult one of the many books or websites on beekeeping. Additionally, many colleges offer courses on beekeeping.

Milkweed Bugs

These small true bugs can be raised in a small fish bowl or jar. In the wild, they feed on milkweed seeds, but in captivity they will adapt to feeding on raw unsalted pumpkin seeds. Offer a few seeds to each bug, and change their food each week or so. Unlike many other insects, milkweed bugs need water above and beyond what they get from their food. One easy way to supply this is in a small test tube with a plug of cotton to serve as a wick.

Milkweed bug eggs are yellow to orange and will hatch in about ten days. As the young grow, you'll need to add some scrunched-up paper towels

Pill Bugs From the Deep

A deep-sea isopod, *Bathynomus giganteus*, lives in the ocean at below a depth of 1,200 feet (366 meters). While they look just like a pill bug, they grow to a length of over 14 inches (35.6 cm) and can only be kept in special coldwater marine aquariums.

for them to climb on. The top of their cage must be secure so that they cannot escape. One method that works well is to cover the top with a piece of thin, loose weave cloth and hold it in place with a large rubber band.

The very similar-looking box elder bug feeds on female box elder trees and so does not live well in captivity. These insects can become pests around some homes when they congregate on the sunny side of the house trying to keep warm. Never call an exterminator about these harmless insects. The only sure way to control them is to remove any box elder trees that are growing near your house.

Pill Bugs

Most crustaceans are aquatic animals such as crabs, shrimp, and lobsters. A

few crustaceans can live on land; one type is the common pill bug (also known as roly-poly bugs, wood lice, sow bugs, potato bugs, and isopods). These small terrestrial arthropods make good pets for beginning hobbyists. Pill bugs look like little armadillos as they crawl around, and they even roll up into a protective ball to avoid predators, just like armadillos. They are easy to find; just look under a rock or rotten log in a forest or in a garden.

Groups of pill bugs can be kept in a small container—they just need some damp sand and soil mixed with some leaf litter to hide under. They undergo incomplete metamorphoses, and after the eggs hatch, the juveniles molt four or five times until they reach their adult size of about 1/2 inch (1.3 cm). They require soft food like bean sprouts, potato, or bits of fruit. Because they are nocturnal and prefer to live underneath things (they are positively thigmotaxic), they are not easy to view as pets. Still, they are hardy and fun to keep, making them a great starter pet.

Aquatic Insects

A hobby very similar to insect keeping is that of home aquarium keeping. Most aquarists keep fish as pets, but if you want to mix the two hobbies, perhaps aquatic insects will

fit the bill. All species need to be kept in a standard aquarium with a filter and a heater, as well as a tight-fitting screen cover. Remove all uneaten food promptly to avoid fouling the water. Change about 20 percent of the water with spring or tap water every two weeks to help to remove dissolved waste products given off by the insects. Because all of these species are highly predatory, they often will try to eat one another and cannot be kept with fish. Remember, adult aquatic insects breathe air, so provide a floating piece of wood or cork bark for your aquatic insects to climb on to breathe.

Diving Bugs

Abedus indentatus and related species

Range: Worldwide.

Habitat: Ponds, streams, and rivers.

Adult Size: 3 inches (7.5 cm) for *Lethoceros* sp.

Diet: Other insects, tadpoles, and small fish.

Housing: Aquarium.

The hickory horned devil is the caterpillar of the royal walnut moth. It is found in North American forests living and feeding on hickory, ash, walnut, and butternut trees.

Environment: 70° to 80°F (21° to 27°C)

Dangers: Can bite.

Diving bugs are predatory insects that are sometimes kept as pets. Highly aggressive, they cannot be kept as a group unless they are fed well. Because they can fly, their aquarium must be tightly covered. They have sharp biting mouthparts that can draw blood if they happen to bite you. Despite these drawbacks, they do fascinate some insect hobbyists, especially those who happen to also have a home aquarium.

The female lays her 50 to 150 eggs on the back of the male, and he incubates them. By carrying the eggs on his back to the surface from time to time, he allows the air to partially dry them. This controls fungi and bacteria that might otherwise attack the eggs. After three weeks, the eggs hatch. Move the pale yellow nymphs to individual containers filled with water and a bit of plant (live or plastic) for them to

cling to. Adults and young alike can be fed on chopped-up frozen crickets. Change the water in the rearing tanks as needed, and remove any moldy cricket parts. The nymphs will go through five instars (molts) during the next three months until they reach adulthood.

Dragonflies and Damselflies
Order Odonata

Range: Worldwide.

Habitat: Larvae found in freshwater streams, ponds, and lakes.

Adult Size: Abdomen length up to 5.5 inches (14 cm).

Diet: Other insects.

Housing: Larvae can be kept in a typical aquarium; adults must be released.

Environment: 70° to 80°F (21° to 27°C).

Dangers: None.

There are more than 5,000 species of damselflies and dragonflies found throughout the world. Adults need huge amounts of room to fly, so they can really only be kept as pets during their submerged larval stage, when they are nymphs. Offer the larvae dead crickets on which to feed and some submerged plant material on which to climb. If you allow some of the plant material to extend up above the surface of the water, the nymphs will use this area to crawl out of the water and molt into their adult form. Release the adults once their wings have dried so that they can fly.

You can feed sunburst diving beetles crickets, mealworms, other small insects, and tropical fish flake food.

Sunburst Diving Beetle

Thermonectus marmoratus

Range: Southwestern United States.

Habitat: Streams and small rivers.

Adult Size: 0.5 inch (1.3 cm).

Diet: Crushed crickets.

Housing: Standard aquarium.

Environment: 70° to 80°F (21° to 27°C).

Dangers: None.

Because these are true beetles, they undergo complete metamorphoses. The female lays her eggs in damp sand (not totally underwater). The eggs hatch into aquatic larva called *water tigers*. The larvae feed on daphnia or other small invertebrates. Eventually, the water tigers burrow into the damp sand again and pupate. The adult beetles then emerge and return to the water.

The formerly named yellow-spotted diving beetle is an example of a case where a single person actually changed the common name of an animal. An insect curator at a zoo maintained a colony of these beautiful beetles and felt that their name did not do them justice. He began calling them "sunburst diving beetles" instead, and soon the name stuck. Only a few entomologists still refer to this species by its old name.

Water Scorpion

Ranatra and *Nepa* spp.

Range: North America, Europe.

Habitat: Slow-moving streams and ponds, even cattle water tanks.

Water scorpion stalking prey. Notice the breathing tube extending off the abdomen.

Adult Size: 2 inches (5 cm).

Diet: Other aquatic insects, daphnia.

Housing: Standard aquarium.

Environment: 70° to 80°F (21° to 27°C).

Dangers: None.

Water scorpions are true insects that cannot sting like real scorpions. They range in shape from very long and slender (like an aquatic stick insect) to short and squat, more like a diving bug. All can be identified by the breathing tubes that extend back from their abdomens. They are often seen holding onto some aquatic plants, head down, with their breathing tube extended to the surface, patiently waiting for some prey item to swim by. Offer them plenty of submerged vegetation (even plastic aquarium plants will work well). Make sure that some plants extend to within 0.5 inches (1.3 cm) of the water surface to allow the water scorpions to reach the surface with their breathing tube.

Bugs That Scurry, Swim, and Fly

Chapter 6

Spiders and Their Kin

This chapter describes the care requirements of all those bugs that are not true insects. There are around 70,000 species of arachnids that include spiders, scorpions, mites, and ticks. All arachnids have eight legs as opposed to the normal six-legged true insects. Also discussed in this chapter are the myriapods, the 500 or so species that make up the group of centipedes and millipedes. While none of these animals are closely related to insects, they are still terrestrial arthropods and so can be kept as pets in much the same way.

Some people have a great fear (or phobia) about spiders and their relatives. While it is true that some of these creatures can bite or sting, most do not, and all can make good pets if properly cared for. Many of these species are long lived, a real bonus for people who keep bugs as pets!

Spiders

Spiders have long been favored pets for those seeking the truly exotic. With more than 40,000 species of spiders in the world, there is obviously a tremendous variety in terms of size, shape, coloration, and habits. Of this group, the tarantulas are the most popular pets. Entire books have been written about the captive care of tarantulas, and for hobbyists interested specifically in those species, buying one of those titles will give more in-depth information than this book can offer. For insect hobbyists who wish to just try their hand at keeping spiders, the following information will serve as a good starting point.

Common Spiders

Cellar Spider
Pholcus phalangioides

Range: North America.

Habitat: Often inside homes.

Adult Size: 2.5-inch (6.5-cm) leg span.

Diet: Small insects and other spiders.

Housing: Simple cage.

Environment: Typical room conditions.

Dangers: None.

This is perhaps the easiest terrestrial arthropod species to acquire as a pet. Most homes have at least a few of these small spiders living in the basement or cellar. They create a tangled web, often in corners of rooms near the ceiling. When agitated, they sway their bodies rapidly back and forth. Some people think that this action blurs the outline of the spider, making it at least partially camouflaged from potential predators.

Cellar spiders are hardy and can live for more than two years in captivity.

FAMILY-FRIENDLY TIP

Arachnophobia

Many people believe that having a fear of spiders is natural and that even babies know to be afraid of these creatures. Actually, the fear of any animal is something that is learned from your parents and peers. Children who are raised with parents who show fear and react badly whenever they see a spider will usually become afraid of them as well. On the other hand, kids who grow up in households that happen to keep bugs as pets will not be as afraid of them as will children whose parents scream and swat at every bug that they see. Please respect all animals, but do not fear them.

Many people kill them when they find them in their homes, but these small spiders can help to control other insects that might otherwise infest a person's home. In Europe, this species is often called the daddy longlegs spider, but in North America, that term is most often used for the harvestman, which is not a spider at all. (See section "Harvestmen.")

Jumping Spiders

Evarcha, Phidippus, Salticus, and related species

Range: Worldwide.

Habitat: Vegetated areas but also inside homes

Adult Size: 0.4 to 0.8 inches (1 to 2 cm).

Diet: Other spiders and small insects.

Housing: Small cage with climbing branches.

Environment: Normal indoor conditions.

Dangers: Very fast, may try to bite (but harmless).

Jumping spiders are one of the most interesting types of spiders to watch. They have very good eyesight and are quick hunters. They are alerted to the movement of small insects nearby; they quickly turn and watch the insect, and when the time is right, they rush in and leap to capture it. Some jumping spiders release a bit of silk just as they jump, using this as a safety cord if they should happen to fall. They live very well in smaller cages and just require a few crickets each week as food. A small bit of damp sponge can

Jumping spiders can be found worldwide; most species are quite easy to keep.

Provide your orb weaver with a large open area in the cage so that it can spin its web.

be offered, but these spiders get most, if not all, of their moisture needs from their food.

Orb Weaver

Argiope and *Nephila* spp.

Range: Worldwide.

Habitat: In branches of plants.

Adult Size: Up to 4-inch (10-cm) diameter leg span.

Diet: Live insects that are caught in their web.

Housing: Large cage with open area to build web.

Environment: Typical indoor conditions for most species.

Dangers: None.

This group of spiders was made famous in the children's book *Charlotte's Web*, with the title character being an orb weaver spider. While these spiders do well in captivity, they require a cage large enough for them to spin their webs—some species need as much as 1 cubic yard of space (0.76 cubic meters).

Adult females will live for many months, but to breed them, you must find a male, and these are very small. One way to start a colony of these spiders is to collect an egg mass and hatch them out inside a screen or glass enclosure. The spiderlings are cannibalistic but will also feed on fruit flies. The trouble is that any males in the group will likely mature before the females do, and the males are not very long lived. This often means that you will need to raise only females from one egg mass and follow that a few months later by a second egg mass from which you raise males to mate the now mature females.

Offer your orb weaver forked branches to form its web, and then watch it feed when you toss a cricket into its web—very interesting! As unpleasant as it sounds, it is best to remove the hind legs from the cricket before placing it into the web. Crickets can kick and tear up a nicely built web very quickly, and then the spider has to spend a lot of time and energy to repair the web.

Wolf Spider

Hogna, *Lycosa*, *Pardosa*, and related spp.

Range: Worldwide.

Habitat: On the ground in fields and woods.

Adult Size: Up to 4-inch (10-cm) leg span in the females of some species.

Diet: Live insects.

Housing: Simple cage with open floor space and some cover to hide under.

Environment: Normal room conditions.

Dangers: May bite if handled but not dangerous.

The 3,000 or so species of wolf spiders are large, hairy, ground-dwelling arachnids usually patterned with a mixture of gray, black, and brown. Females of most species carry their eggs with them in a round egg sac made of their silk and attached to their spinnerets. After the eggs hatch, the spiderlings may be carried on the females' backs for up to a month as they grow.

Wolf spiders are hardy and long lived; some females have been reported to live for up to three years in captivity. They should be offered water to drink (from a soaked sponge in a dish) and can be fed crickets or other soft-bodied

Useful Tools

Long forceps (tweezers) are useful when working with any terrestrial arthropod that tries to bite. They can be used to remove water containers for cleaning, to move cage decorations around, or even to push the creature out of the way so that you can reach in to perform some other maintenance task in the cage. There are two common types of forceps available: stainless steel medical forceps and plastic aquarium tongs. Both have benefits and drawbacks. The metal varieties are more expensive, but the plastic tongs are not as sturdy. In most cases, don't use forceps to pick up an animal directly unless you have great control or you may crush and injure the specimen. The only exception is with some larger species, such as scorpions, which can be gently lifted by their tail. Fish net also can be used to move arthropods around, but some species with spines may get caught up in the netting material.

One interesting behavior of wolf spiders is that the females carry their eggs and young on their backs.

insects as often as they will eat (usually one or two prey items per week). Never leave any food animals in with a wolf spider if it does not immediately consume them. Reports are that even crickets or grasshoppers may turn on a wolf spider if left in with it too long.

Fisher spiders (*Dolomedes* sp.) and nursery-web spiders (*Pisaurina* sp.) look very similar to wolf spiders, and some of them can be cared for in much the same way. Fishing spiders have the interesting habit of hanging head-down near water, waiting to grab small aquatic insects that happen to swim by.

Tarantulas

Tarantulas are large, fearsome spiders that have huge fangs and can give a painful yet rarely dangerous bite. Some species are more aggressive than others

are, but all should be handled with care (or better yet, not at all). It is possible that some obscure species will have more toxic venom—the strength of all species' venom is not known with certainty. In addition to their ability to bite, New World tarantulas (those from the Americas) are capable of shedding fine urticating hairs from the top of their abdomens by flicking their legs against them. These hairs have barbs on them and can imbed themselves in the skin (or more seriously, the throat or eyes) of humans. In the skin, these hairs can cause burning and itching—similar to that caused by strands of fiberglass. If you have ever seen a "bald" tarantula, this simply means that the animal has shed most of its urticating hairs and is not necessarily an indication of old age.

Although there are a couple of possible exceptions (like some *Avicularia* sp. tarantulas), all tarantulas must be kept separately, in individual cages. They are only brought together for mating, a complicated topic outside the scope of this manual.

Mexican Red-Kneed Tarantula
Brachypelma smithi

Range: Mexico.

Habitat: Scrublands.

Adult Size: Up to 6-inch (15-cm) leg span.

Diet: Crickets and other insects.

Housing: Singly in a moderate-sized cage.

Environment: 77°F (25°C) and over 50% relative humidity.

Dangers: May bite, urticating hairs.

This species is one of the most popular pet tarantulas. Colorful and relatively docile, they make excellent pets. Females can live longer than 20 years in captivity, but males may die soon after their final molt at just a few years in age. Always try to acquire a female unless your plan is to try to breed them. You will likely need the help of an expert to tell a male from a female, as the differences between the two are very slight. Red-knees and many other species of tarantula live in burrows, so providing them with a small section of cork bark to crawl under will make them feel more secure.

The habits and care requirements of the closely related Mexican red-leg (*Brachypelma emilia*) are virtually the same as for the red-knee. (In fact, some

Note the bald patch on the back of this red-kneed tarantula. This is one of the species that can kick off irritating hairs.

Brown recluses are dangerous spiders that the average bug hobbyist should not keep. Unfortunately, they are difficult to identify accurately.

people often reverse the common names for these animals.) Both species require permits before sending them between two different countries. When the choice is available, always buy captive-raised tarantulas because this protects wild populations.

Rose-Haired Tarantula

Grammostola rosea

Range: Southern Peru and Chile.

Habitat: Desert scrubland.

Adult Size: 6-inch (15-cm) leg span.

Diet: Crickets or other soft-bodied insects.

Housing: Moderate-sized cage with vermiculite and potting soil substrate.

Environment: 77°F (25°C) and under 50% relative humidity.

Dangers: May bite, urticating hairs.

This common, hardy species of tarantula is found in a few different color varieties (called morphs). Most are available as wild-caught adults, so always make sure that the animal you buy has begun to adapt to captivity. Avoid any tarantula that is missing portions of a leg or that has a thin abdomen. These are usually very docile and hardy tarantulas, but there is tremendous variability in the temperament of this species.

Spiders to Avoid

Black Widow

This well-known venomous spider (and related species of the genus *Latrodectus*) is widespread throughout the United States and other parts of the world. Females grow to almost 2 inches (5 cm) in diameter and have a large abdomen that usually has a red or orange mark on its underside. Widows are normally found in wood or debris piles or in outbuildings (In fact, in days gone by, almost half of all black widow bites were from people accidentally sitting on one when using an outhouse). Rarely found indoors, they are sometimes seen in a basement or crawlspace.

Their venom is highly neurotoxic, but because such a small amount is injected when the females bite, less than 1 percent of people who are bitten by a black widow spider (and who receive medical attention) end up dying. First aid for a bite must include keeping calm and immediately contacting emergency medical personnel. An ice pack applied to the bite may temporarily help to relieve some of the pain.

Brown Recluse

This species, as well as ten other members of the genus *Loxoceles*, is probably the most commonly misidentified spider species. Many people simply call every small brown spider a brown recluse. In reality, this species is difficult to positively identify. The well-known violin mark on their bodies may be faint or nonexistent. The most reliable way to identify spiders of this genus is to count their eyes using a magnifying lens. Recluse spiders have six eyes, arranged in pairs in a semicircle on their head (cephalothorax); most other spiders

Urban Legend: Dangerous Daddy Longlegs

The Internet is filled with factual errors, and some of these develop over time into urban legends. One such story is that the common daddy longlegs are the most venomous spider in the world, but their fangs are too short to pierce human skin. First of all, these animals (also called harvestmen) are not spiders at all; they belong to the order Phalangida. Secondly, they do not possess harmful venom, even if they did manage to bite through our skin. It makes for a good story, but it simply isn't true!

have eight eyes. The brown recluse is most commonly found in the south-central United States, and they prefer damp, dark habitats.

Symptoms of a brown recluse bite range from a minor localized reaction to severe tissue damage (necrosis). Unless the spider is actually seen to have caused the bite, people must keep in mind that there are many

The infamous black widow.

hobo spiders (*Tegenaria* sp.) has been implicated in causing reactions in humans who have been bitten by them. Native to Europe, these spiders have been introduced into some areas of the western United States.

Sac spiders (family Clubionidae) are common nocturnal spiders in some homes. They superficially resemble brown recluse spiders, and their bite can cause similar (but much less serious) tissue damage. Sac spiders usually bite when trapped between a person's skin and their clothing.

There are other exotic species of spiders such as the Sydney funnel web that can be dangerous to humans. Always treat any unknown tropical spider as having the potential to be dangerous to humans.

other disease problems that can cause identical reactions, including bites and stings from other insects (if they become infected), as well as a variety of bacterial, viral, and fungal skin infections.

Hobo Spiders and Others

From time to time, reports on the Internet indicate that the group of

Harvestmen

Also called daddy longlegs, harvestmen look like spiders but in fact are merely close relatives. They are arachnids but belong to the order Opiliones and not Araneae, as do true spiders. The most obvious difference between spiders and harvestmen is that the latter has a single body segment in which the cephalothorax and the abdomen are fused together. In true spiders, you can usually see a separate, very distinct abdomen. There is a spider that

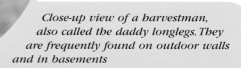

Close-up view of a harvestman, also called the daddy longlegs. They are frequently found on outdoor walls and in basements

is also called the daddy longlegs; this is the common house spider, *Pholcus* sp., discussed in the previous section.

Harvestmen are commonly found around houses, so seeking them out is usually a simple matter. Collecting them is another issue. Although relatively slow, they do have the habit of dropping their legs when disturbed. These legs will twitch for some time, and it is thought that perhaps this serves as a distraction for predators, allowing the harvestman to escape. To avoid damaging them, try to usher them gently into a container rather than picking them up by hand or in a net.

Harvestmen are typically seasonal creatures, laying eggs that then overwinter, hatching out in the spring. They are relatively hardy in captivity but do best when housed by themselves. Two males may fight one another, and if kept with other animals, they will either try to eat them or be eaten, depending on the species. Captive care can be quite simple—they do well at room temperate in just in a small container with a bit of moist tissue paper as a water supply. Most harvestmen species are omnivorous, feeding on a variety of plant and animal material. While they will feed on small living insects, they usually cannot attack and kill something as large as even a juvenile cricket, so you will usually need to crush a cricket every few days and offer them that as food.

For variety you can try feeding them some vegetable matter from time to time, like tomatoes, fruit, or anything with a high moisture content. Cleaning their enclosure can be problematic as it is during handling that they can so easily become damaged. One easy method is to have two identical cages that open at the top. When it is time to clean one, just hold the containers up mouth to mouth and gently incline one and try to maneuver the harvestmen into the clean container.

Scorpions and Their Relatives

There are 1,400 species of true scorpion and another 100 species of whip scorpion, many of which make good pet bugs. These large arachnids have a cephalothorax (main body) with four pairs of walking legs and a pair of large pedipalps with pincers in the front. Scorpions have a mobile tail with a stinger at the end, while whip scorpions, as their name implies, have

Like other scorpions, female emperor scorpions carry their babies on their back until they can fend for themselves.

a whip-like appendage for a tail. Most species are nocturnal, and almost all are ground dwelling—some even make burrows.

Scorpions often require warmer temperatures than are found in the typical household, so they need some type of supplemental heat. Heat lamps, which work well for many other pet bugs, are not appreciated by these nocturnal creatures. Pet stores sell special heat mats that are designed to fit under an aquarium and gently heat the entire enclosure. Care needs to be taken in their use with scorpions; these animals naturally burrow to escape warm temperatures. If they do this in a cage with a heat mat installed, they will be brought even closer to the heat source and may die. When using a heat mat with scorpions (or other burrowing arthropods), it is important to only have the mat installed on one-half of the cage. That way, should the temperature grow too warm, the

creature can burrow in the substrate away from the heat source.

True Scorpions

Emperor Scorpion
Pandinus imperator

Range: Tropical West Africa.

Habitat: Rainforests.

Adult Size: 6 inches (15.2 cm).

Diet: Live crickets, mealworms.

Housing: Cage with open floor space, layer of mulch or potting soil, cork bark.

Environment: 77° F (25°C) and over 50% relative humidity.

Dangers: May sting or pinch if mishandled.

This is one of the most docile scorpions. Because they are also very large, they make impressive pets. Although wild-caught specimens are routinely available, always try to find captive-raised scorpions to buy. These will already be adapted to captive life, and some people think that emperor scorpions are being overcollected in Africa for the pet trade. Emperor scorpions need a small bowl of fresh water to drink from and should be fed crickets a few times each week. Watch for overeating; you can judge a fat scorpion because its body plates will grow apart, showing lighter-colored tissue between them.

Other Species

Asian forest scorpions (*Heterometrus* sp.) are sometimes offered for sale. These look very similar to emperor scorpions, but they are a little more aggressive. Their care requirements are the same, however.

The desert hairy scorpion (*Hadrurus arizonensis*) is a large scorpion found in the American Southwest. Growing up to 5 inches (12.7 cm) long, they require very dry, warm conditions. Although they are aggressive, their sting is not usually dangerous to humans.

Related Bugs

Vinegaroon

Mastigoproctus giganteus

Range: Southwestern US.

Habitat: Burrowing species, dry scrubland.

Adult Size: Up to 6 inches (15.2 cm) including their whip-like tail.

Diet: Live crickets and mealworms.

Housing: Cage with ample floor space, soil to burrow in, and cork bark to hide under.

Environment: 77°F (25°C) and under 40% relative humidity.

Dangers: Can release acetic acid from pores on abdomen.

These nocturnal arachnids are popular pet species because they are simple to care for and do not have a

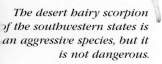

The desert hairy scorpion of the southwestern states is an aggressive species, but it is not dangerous.

Vinegaroons get their name from their defensive behavior of releasing acetic acid from pores in the abdomen.

stinger like true scorpions. Vinegaroons have strong leg-like pedipalps that are formed into pincers, and they do not hesitate to pinch with them if they are handled. If they are kept under very dry conditions, they will attempt to conserve moisture by burying down into the substrate and remaining there. Always have a shallow dish of water for this species to drink from. This allows them to regulate their moisture needs easily.

Giant Tailless Whip Scorpion

Damon variegatus

Range: Africa: Tanzania and Kenya.

Habitat: Trees and shrubs.

Adult Size: 8-inch (20.3-cm) leg span (tip to tip); 3-inch (7.6-cm) body length.

Diet: Crickets and other live insects.

Housing: Tall aquarium with climbing structures.

Environment: Warm (80°F [26°C]) with moderate humidity.

Dangers: Nervous animal, fast and skittish. May pinch if handled.

Occasionally available as wild-caught adults imported from Tanzania, this species makes a unique pet for the serious hobbyist. This is a very fragile species that should not be handled. During the molting process, they may damage their long thin legs if not given enough room to spread out while emerging from their old skin.

This timid species will hide if given an opportunity to do so. One method to entice them to be more visible is to set up a terrarium with a flat piece of cork bark lying upright against the front glass. By installing a bright light above the terrarium (shining down on the back of the bark), the whip scorpion will naturally move to the dimmer area, in plain sight next to the front glass. They should be fed live

The Secret for Glowing Skin

Many scorpions will glow (fluoresce) a pale greenish-yellow or blue color when exposed to long wave ultraviolet light (black light). While this is an interesting observation, do not expose these animals to this type of light for very long because it may stress them. (They stop glowing after a few weeks, which indicates that the exposure to this type of light is causing changes in their skin.) A portable ultraviolet light can be used to help to locate scorpions in the wild—they glow so brightly when illuminated that it makes them much easier to see. Only the adults glow, which may indicate that this feature is used in mate recognition.

adult crickets or other feeder insects two to three times per week. Misting is only required in very dry households; supplemental heat is important.

Centipedes and Millipedes

This group is interesting in that it contains one of the easiest to handle of all species of terrestrial arthropod (the giant millipede), as well as one that simply cannot be handled at all (the giant centipede). Centipedes are quick nocturnal predators, possessing a venomous bite. Millipedes are slower, and they are either strict herbivores or they feed on decaying matter.

Some species of millipede are reportedly capable of releasing hydrogen cyanide gas through pores in their exoskeleton, while others release liquid organic acids. Both behaviors are techniques they use to drive away potential predators. In some cases, millipedes will release these compounds when handled roughly by humans. If this happens, simply wash your hands and there is likely to be no serious skin reaction.

Giant centipedes (*Scolopendra* sp.) are fast and aggressive and can give a very painful bite with their oversized mandibles. Their venom does not usually cause life-threatening reactions in humans, but because the bite is so painful and freely given, they must never be handled.

House Centipede

Scutigera coleoptrata and related species

Range: Worldwide in temperate regions.

Tailless whip scorpions are found in the tropics worldwide. Most of those offered for sale are from Africa.

Habitat: Often inside homes.

Adult Size: Possibly up to 2 inches (5 cm) total length.

Diet: Small insects such as pinhead crickets.

Housing: Small cage with some climbing structures.

Environment: Normal indoor conditions.

Dangers: May try to bite but not dangerous.

The common house centipede, with its 15 pairs of very long legs and fast, scurrying behavior, has the tendency to frighten many people when found inside their homes. Although considered a house pest by most, these arthropods serve a purpose: They feed on other insects living in your home that you would be even less inclined to want to see (cockroaches and silverfish,

for example). This species can live a surprisingly long three to five years in captivity. Collect house centipedes carefully so that they do not lose their legs.

Giant Centipedes

Scolopendra heros, S. subspinipes, and related spp.

Range: The Americas and Asia.

Habitat: Tropical and subtropical regions.

Adult Size: 8 inches (20.3 cm); up to 12 inches (30.5 cm) maximum for some species.

Diet: Crickets, cockroaches.

Housing: Secure cage with soil to burrow in.

Environment: 77°F (25°C) and over 50% relative humidity.

Dangers: Will bite; bite very painful, with one fatality recorded.

There are many species of giant centipede offered for sale, and most have identical care requirements. The only real difference is that you need to know if the species you have is from a desert area or if it is from a tropical wet forest area. This will, in turn, tell you how much moisture the animal will prefer. All giant centipedes should be offered water in a shallow dish, but the desert species can be kept on a dry soil/sand substrate, while the tropical forest species should be given slightly damp soil in which to burrow.

Giant centipedes have very powerful mandibles that can chew through many types of plastic screen tops. It is best to use a glass aquarium with a tight-fitting top made of steel screen material to house these creatures. The rule is only one giant centipede per cage to avoid cannibalism. Some people recommend that giant centipedes be fed live baby mice once a month or so, but this does not seem to be necessary. Centipedes can live for many years fed solely on crickets and other insects.

North American Millipedes
Narceus americana and related species

Range: North America.

Habitat: Temperate forests.

Adult Size: Varies by species, from 1 to 4 inches (2.5 to 10 cm).

Diet: Varies by species; try fruit, mushrooms, and leaf litter.

Housing: Small terrarium with moist soil and cork bark or leaves to hide under.

Environment: Room temperature, over 50% relative humidity.

Dangers: Some may have irritating skin secretions.

Slow-moving millipedes can easily be captured by hand; just look underneath rotting logs or in piles of decaying leaves. A frightened millipede will simply curl up pinwheel fashion and hope that you will leave it alone. The only real problem with keeping millipedes that you catch yourself

103

Spiders and Their Kin

Legs, Legs, and More Legs

The name *centipede* translates from Latin to mean *100 feet*. Centi- is a prefix meaning *100* (as in 100 cents). The suffix *–pede* as a suffix means *foot*. (A *pede*strian is someone who walks.) Centipedes possess between 30 and 70 legs (with a few species having 180 pairs), one pair on each body segment.

It is often stated that millipedes have 1,000 legs because the word *millipede* translates to *1,000 feet*. However, most millipedes have only a few hundred legs, with the most being about 750. Millipedes have two pairs of legs on each of their body segments. The more segments a species has, the more legs.

is that you may not know exactly what type of food it needs. As with many bugs that you catch yourself, you will often find them living amongst the food they prefer to eat. Therefore, if you find a millipede living near some fungi or moldy leaves, chances are that is also its food. If you do not see your millipede accepting any foods that you offer it, return it to where you captured it. Always remember to replace logs, stones, and other hiding places *exactly* as you find them. This preserves the environment for the animals that call that place their home.

Giant African Millipede

Archispirostreptus (Graphidostreptus) gigas

Range: Tropical Western Africa.

Habitat: Rainforest; burrows in damp soil.

Adult Size: 11 inches (28 cm).

Diet: Bananas, melons, romaine lettuce, cucumbers, apples, and other fruits and vegetables.

Housing: Simple terrarium with soil substrate and cork bark to hide under.

Environment: 77°F (25°C) and over 50% relative humidity.

Dangers: Skin secretions that can stain and irritate skin.

These large, docile millipedes are the best bug pets for children. They are long lived and relatively inexpensive. One interesting note is that they also can be kept in groups and can even be kept with Madagascar hissing cockroaches, another popular pet bug. Giant millipedes frequently reproduce in captivity. Although some people report that they have raised

House centipedes are common in homes, making them already adapted to captivity.

An Arizona giant centipede.

baby millipedes in the same cage as the adults, it is best to remove the babies to their own smaller container where you can keep a better eye on them. Feeding the babies is the same as for the adults, and as they molt, they gradually turn darker in color until they become the same dark color as the adults. Take care if you are trying to breed millipedes because changing the substrate will also remove any incubating eggs.

Because this species rarely climbs, floor space of the cage is more important than its height. Sometimes colonies of these millipedes become infested with tiny mites. These do not seem to harm the giant millipede, so if they become bothersome to you, gently wipe them off the millipede's body with a damp cloth or small paintbrush.

Never use any insecticides or chemicals to remove these mites—the same chemicals may harm the millipede itself.

The taxonomy of these pet millipedes is not well known. There is another species from Africa that is slightly smaller and has a more reddish color that also does well in captivity. There are also some giant millipedes from Asia that live very well. However, some species imported as pets do not seem to thrive, including the Madagascar pill millipede and various species known as Tanzanian flame millipedes. It is likely that the failure of these species in captivity is due to their needing some special type of food that cannot be offered them in captivity.

Spiders and Their Kin

Glossary

abdomen: the rear section of a terrestrial arthropod's body, behind the thorax or cephalothorax.

aposematic coloration: bright coloration or strong patterning of an animal that warns potential predators that the animal has some sort of defense. The bright yellow and black stripes of a wasp serve as such a warning.

arachnid: spiders, scorpions, ticks, and mites.

arthropod: an invertebrate animal with jointed legs and an exoskeleton.

cephalothorax: a body section of arachnids that consists of the head and thorax fused together.

cerci: a pair of protuberances from the end of the abdomen of some arthropods. *Scolopendra* centipedes have well-developed cerci.

chelicerae: fang-like appendages on the front of the cephalothorax of arachnids.

chrysalis: A protective skin that encases a developing pupa as it metamorphoses from a larva to an adult butterfly. A *cocoon* is functionally the same but is formed by moths as they develop.

colony: a group of social insects in which each member has specific functions that support the needs of the group, such as food gathering, defense, and reproduction. Honeybees are an example of a colonial insect species.

ecdysis: the process of shedding off the exoskeleton of an arthropod to allow for increasing the animal's size as it grows.

elytra: the hard, often shiny and colorful first pair of wings that cover the delicate flying wings when a beetle is at rest.

exoskeleton: a hard, external skin-like skeleton possessed by all arthropods. Sometimes called the cuticle.

family: a biological classification below that of an order, consisting of a group of related genera.

frass (also fras): waste products of terrestrial arthropods. This may be feces, shed exoskeletons, uneaten food particles, or liquids expelled during metamorphosis.

genus (plural: genera): a biological classification above the level of species and below that of family. Species in the same genus are very similar but usually cannot interbreed.

imago: the adult stage of an insect that has completed its metamorphosis.

larva (plural: larvae): an early life stage of an arthropod, often wormlike in appearance, usually very different than the final adult form.

metamorphosis: the change in body form that occurs as some animal species develop. Complete metamorphosis contains an egg stage, which hatches into a larva, which then encloses as a pupa, which finally opens and the adult insect emerges. Incomplete metamorphosis is seen in mantids, walking sticks, and grasshoppers, in which the change from juvenile to adult is less pronounced.

nymph: the juvenile stage of any insect that undergoes incomplete or gradual metamorphosis. Nymphs of aquatic insects such as dragonflies are sometimes called naiads.

ootheca: a group of insect eggs collected in a mass. Often deposited by cockroaches and praying mantids. The covering around the eggs protects them from some predators, as well as from cold weather.

ovipositor: A structure at the end of some female insects used to deposit eggs, usually into soil or some plant structure.

pedipalp: small leg-like organs near the mouth of spiders and their relatives that are used to sense their environment and to hold their prey. In insects, similar structures are called maxillary palps.

phylum: a primary division in the classification of organisms just below kingdom.

pronotum: the top covering of the first segment of an insect's thorax.

saprophyte: an organism that gains food energy from nonliving organic material.

species: a biological classification below the level of genus. Typically comprising organisms that can interbreed and that are found in geographic proximity.

thorax: middle body segment of insects where the legs and wings attach.

thigmotaxic: an animal's reaction to being in tight spaces. Cockroaches are positively thigmotaxic because they prefer to have their body in contact with the surfaces around them. Butterflies are negatively thigmotaxic because they do not like to be in contact with surfaces (other than their feet).

urticating hairs: irritating hairs on the bodies of most new world tarantulas and some caterpillars that can embed themselves in a person's skin. This is a protection against predators who might try to eat them.

Resources

Articles and Books

Hemdal, J.F., Cypher, J. 2006. "Crustacean Nation." *Marine Fish and Reef USA Annual* 8(1):78-85

Hemdal, J.F. 1996. "Butterfly: What's in a name?" *Safari* 4(2):4.

Kneidel, Sally. 1994. *Pet Bugs.* San Francisco, California: Jossey-Bass, Inc.

Kneidel, Sally 1999. *More Pet Bugs.* New York, New York: Jossey-Bass, Inc.

McGavin, George C. 2000. *Insects, Spiders, and Other Terrestrial Arthropods.* New York, New York: Dorling Kindersley, Inc.

Clubs and Societies

The Amateur Entomologists' Society,
PO Box 8774,
London,
SW7 5ZG
E-mail: contact@amentsoc.org
www.amensoc.org/index.htm

American Arachnological Society
Department of Entomology
University of Maryland
College Park, MD 20742
Telephone: (301) 405-7519
Fax: (301) 314-9290
E-mail: jshultz@umd.edu
www.americanarachnology.org/

American Tarantula Society
PO Box 756
Carlsbad, NM 88221
Telephone: (505) 885-8406
E-mail: spiderbob@atshq.org
www.atshq.org/

Entomological Society of America
10001 Derekwood Lane, Suite 100
Lanham, MD 20706-4876
Telephone: (301) 731-4535
Fax: (301) 731-4538
E-mail: esa@entsoc.org
www.entsoc.org/index.htm

Entomological Society of Canada
393 Winston Avenue
Ottawa, Ontario, Canada K2A 1Y8
Telephone: (613) 725-2619
Fax: (613) 725-9349
E-mail: entsoc.can@bellnet.ca
www.esc-sec.org/

Websites

Allpet Roaches
www.angelfire.com/oh2/Roaches

Bug Bios
www.insects.org/

BugGuide
www.bugguide.net/node/view/15740

The Butterfly Website
http://butterflywebsite.com/index.htm

The Dragonfly Website
http://dragonflywebsite.com/articles/
index.htm

Insecta Inspecta World
http://www.insecta-inspecta.com/

Koday's Kids Amazing Insects
www.ivyhall.district96.k12.il.us/4TH/
KKHP/1insects/bugmenu.html

The Phasmid Study Group
http://www.stickinsect.org.uk

The Spider Myths Site
http://www.washingon.edu/
burkemuseum/spidermyth/index.html

The Tarantula Refuge
http://www.angelfire.com/anime/
spiderchris

Wayne's Word entry on beetles
http://waynesword.palomar.edu/
ww0502.htm

What's That Bug?
www.whatsthatbug.com

Index

Index

Acknowledgements

I would like to extend my sincere appreciation to all the people who helped me with this effort: My wife and son, for their patience as I wrote in my home office, night after night. My employer, The Toledo Zoo has always been extremely supportive of my writing efforts. The insect care staff at the Toledo Zoo has always been eager to help with my projects and has offered many excellent suggestions over the years. Finally, I would like to thank my parents, John and Sally, who nurtured my early awareness of animal life despite their having absolutely no interest in the topic of insects in captivity themselves!

About the Author

Jay F. Hemdal has been an avid aquarist and pet owner for over 40 years. He was raised in Ann Arbor, Michigan and set up his first marine aquarium when he was 9 years old. He worked part time for 10 years at various local retail pet stores and fish wholesale companies. After graduating from college, he managed the aquarium department of a large retail pet store for five years until 1985 when he was hired as an aquarist/diver (and later department manager) for the John G. Shedd Aquarium in Chicago. In 1989, he accepted the position of curator of fishes and invertebrates for the Toledo Zoo, where he still works today. In 1996, Jay developed the living terrestrial arthropod collection for the Toledo Zoo which now comprises over 25 exhibits and well over 1000 animals. Jay has written over 100 magazine articles and four books since 1981. He lives with his wife Tammy and their son John Thomas in their home on the bank of the tranquil Raisin River, where they enjoy fishing, archery, and kayaking.

Photo Credits

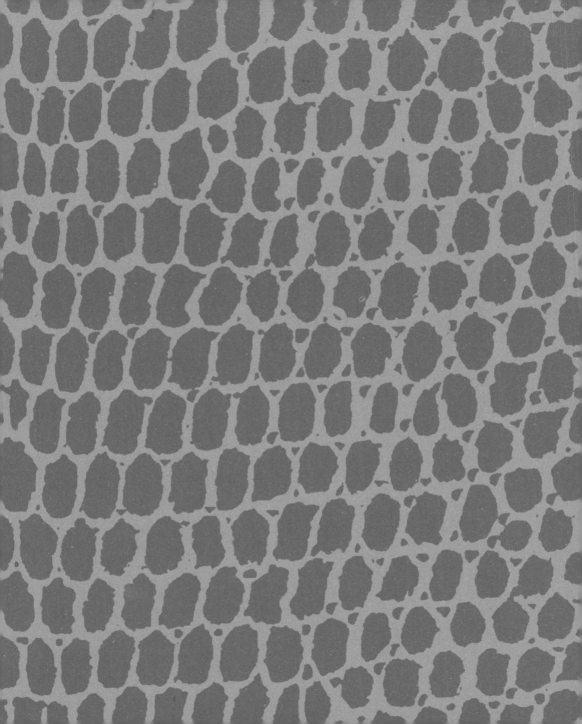